YOUTH
IN SOUTH AND CENTRAL ASIA
A DISCOURSE OF CHANGES
AND CHALLENGES

YOUTH

IN SOUTH AND CENTRAL ASIA

A DISCOURSE OF CHANGES AND CHALLENGES

TAREAK **RATHER** & ASLAM **BHAT**

PARTRIDGE

A Penguin Random House Company

To order additional copies of this book, contact
Partridge India
000 800 10062 62
www.partridgepublishing.com/india
orders.india@partridgepublishing.com

Contents

List of Tables

List of Figures

PREFACE

Youth has long been associated with future hopes, promises of life and the progress of modernity. There is a view that young people of today are more public spirited, socially conscious, and unbound by the vested interest of the adult. They alone can help catch up the world of tomorrow. Simultaneously however, it is also held that youth is a period of strong change characterized by 'open psychic structures', when one is wide open to all sorts of influences. Being curious, the young person is prepared to test out all things—even the forbidden. Moral and other taboos are weakened, established boundaries are transgressed, and this often leads to actions that adults have difficulties accepting. Therefore, that is why anxiety about social change is linked so particularly to youth; modernization, otherwise actually effects the whole population.

Aware of this concern, large number of explanations have been advanced by social scientists towards understanding the behaviour of young people. However, for various reasons, the focus of research has been more on urban youth or student youth or youth of major cities; and youth including rural, tribal, and of remotest areas have been neglected to large extent. Realizing the magnitude of this gap in literature on youth in India, specifically in the context of Jammu and Kashmir, this book present a modest attempt to understand the nature and direction of social change among youth in Ladakh.

As such, the first and second chapters of this book discuss some of the major aspects of the youth transitions and youth culture of Ladakh in the changing social scenario. It is based on the findings of an empirical study of a sample of 150 youth drawn from the Leh in Ladakh, Jammu and Kashmir. The aspects of the sub-culture, as distinctive of the contemporary youth in Ladakh, discussed in this book are the youth's economic situation, educational status, perspective on education, occupational aspirations, occupational mobility, spatial mobility, interests and leisure time activities, dress and food habits, conflict with parents, and premarital sex. The present youth in Ladakh have their outlook on education, employment, social reproduction, and life experiences and interests. Their notion about education reflects the modern attitudes based on economic and market demands, and belief in professional/technical training. Regarding employment, many of them want to leave their native place to seek jobs in big cities or even abroad, and achieve success in their career. They have their preferences for dress and food habits, and views on premarital sex. On the whole, youth in Ladakh have shown the tendency to be as much part of the modern world as the youth elsewhere in the country.

Moreover, this book builds upon some of the major current debates in sociology, specifically youth studies. Ranging from the perspectives on globalisation to "individualisation thesis," the book debates that contemporary discursive interpretations of youth transitions have been extensively influenced by a sociological preoccupation with 'individualisation'—signifying a freeing up of established patterns of transitions and fluid identities. By repercussion, youth researchers have specifically shown an inclination to present the homogeneous and synchronized portraits of contemporary youth, skipping the crucial underlying structural features that still persist and sustain differential transitions into adulthood. Drawing on the in-depth interviews with young people in Kashmir and using the Bourdieu's conceptualisation of interdependent forms of capital, the submission of arguments made in the fourth chapter of book seek to support the proposition that making rational choices and decisions, which constitute individualisation, are still heavily dependent on one's class position. Our evidences suggest that continuing class or habitus based transmission of advantages or disadvantages can't simply be ignored as some proponents of 'individualisation thesis' suggest, rather class analysis still remains a central analytical element in the sociological toolbox.

Against this backdrop chapter 5th further takes on this debate with a special focus on globalisation and mental health of youth in two *giants* of South Asia—India and China. It is argued that globalization and its related social, cultural, and economic changes have significant mental health outcomes for young people. However, mental health disorders among youth are seldom included in the range of problems linked to globalization. It is imperative that these multifaceted associations are considered in light of the substantial and increasing burden of disease caused by mental illness, particularly in Asian countries, which are comparatively young and in next few decades will be the major sources of the growth of world's young population. The evidence reviewed in this chapter makes an argument that globalization has increased [relative] poverty and deprivation, social and income inequality, migration, occupational stress, educational competition, and educated unemployment in India and China. Simultaneously there is evidence which shows that these variables are causally linked with mental health of young people. Altogether, these phenomena are accompanied by higher rates of suicide among lower class, migrant, and student youth. This substantiates the proposition that globalization has significant consequences for the mental health of young people. Some interventions for debate and discussion are considered.

Nonetheless, chapter 6th, 7th and 8th present the scenario of Central Asian youth. When the Soviet Union disintegrated, many Central Asian young people saw their world turned upside down, as their status reduced and their financial and political future became uncertain. In these chapters we have attempted to examine and explore this dilemma, which confronts the majority of young people in contemporary Central Asia, particularly in Uzbekistan. Procedurally, our analysis for the most part incorporates discussions about post-Soviet transition in general and youth transition in particular. We begin with a discussion, considering the evidence on educational opportunities and obstacles in the region. Seventh chapter deals with issues of language politics and predicaments of minority youth in post-Soviet Central Asia and then move onto the issues of unemployment and labour migration, with a special focus on the role of transnational social capital in the transnational migratory processes in the region, and then we conclude by exploring some policy implications that can be drawn from our analysis.

The chapter fourth and fifth, of this book have been drawn from our previously published material. Chapter fourth was originally published in the journal *South Asia Research*. Fifth chapter come from the sources originally published in the journal *Asian Social Work and Policy Review*. In selecting these articles we have been guided by the measure of their present relevance and we hope, the articles reprinted herein would retain the interest of readers today. We have made few changes; nonetheless most of the arguments of these articles are unchanged.

Tareak A. Rather & Mohd Aslam Bhat

1

Youth from Concept to Practice
India in Focus

Youth as an important age category has been recognized throughout the world and history. The conceptualisations of youth and the notions people have of the stages in the life-course of an individual differ from time to time, region to region and culture to culture. There is a considerable variation in the use of the term youth throughout history. For Aristotle and for all antiquity, there were only three stages in the life-course of an individual: childhood, youth and old age. In Aristotle's usage youth is any age from about seven to forty or even forty five (Yedla, 1989: IX). Similarly Rousseau, a French scholar is said to have used the term youth as "young person" (Misra and Jain, 1975: 9).

Unlikely in the traditional Indian context this variation in the concept of the stages in the life-course of an individual has to be seen in terms of Brahmanic model. The Brahmanic model for the various stages of life is given by the concept of the four *Asramas*[1]: *Brahmacharya, Grihastha, Vanaprastha* and *Sanyasa*. The exact age at which the stage of Brahmacharya begins is not fixed and the age at which it ends is not clearly specified though generally it is considered that the period of serious duty begins at the age of eight years (Gore, 1977: 4-5). Nevertheless, it is known that the period of Brahmacharya ends when a person enters on the life of a householder, a Grihasta. Obviously, then the stage of Brahmacharya extends up to the age of eighteen to twenty years. In the terminology of the traditional Indian society the period of "youth" is then co-terminous with the stage of Brahmacharya—at least for the Brahmin and Brahmanised caste groups.

As such, different societies have different terms to refer to and conceptualize the stages in the life-course of an individual. In Arab societies the term *Murahaqa* is used for adolescence and youth in academic texts, and in common language the term *Fata/ Fatat* (masculine and feminine forms) or *Shabb/ Shabba* are used for young boys and girls (Brown *et al.,* 2002: 4-6) respectively, which signify marital status or level of responsibility for or obligation to others. These terms are also indicative of important dimensions of the adolescent period in Arab societies and capture the laypersons perception

---

[1]   *Asramas*-Stages in the progress through life. *Vanaprastha* is the stage when the house holder, having discharged his duties, retires to the forest, preparatory to renunciation of worldly goods. In *Sanyasa* he renounces all possessions except his loin cloth, begging bowl and water pot and lives by begging (see Gore, 1977: 4-5).

of adolescence as loaded with sexual temptations, a period in which adults must closely supervise activities of young ones. Moreover, there is the youth orientation in Muslim societies, which is drawn from holy *Quran*. Youth in Islam is perceived as a raw material to be mobilized, brought up and educated. Youth are active and by being active the youth keep youthful.

Nonetheless, speaking sociologically, youth is a special age category, a time of life, but also a context. It is not a biological notion, as for instance puberty is concerned. It is rather a sociological concept: an attitudinal system and a behavioural pattern related to a specific position in society (United Nations, 1986: 10-11). This is not to deny the relationship between sociological and biological forces, but merely to distinguish them. Any age category—for instance childhood, youth and old age, as Aristotle maintained the three ages of man—is predicated upon biological facts, yet is structured by social forces. It is this process of socialization that is so different from moment to moment, society to society and culture to culture, yet the very fact of socialization upon a given biological group gives rise to a set of partially shared perceptions and problems, which among other things contribute to the creation of a common identity. Youth is the generic notion used to describe this common identity.

To make things more elaborated, the vast sociological literature on youth comprising the works by such sociologists as E.Erikson, K.L.Allerbeck, E.Spranger, T.Parson, K.Mannheim, Rosenmayr Leopold, J.A Perez Islas, L.Garrido and S.N Eisenstadt (Kuczynski *et al.* 1988: 6-7) describe youth in a rather formal manner as: a category of chronological age; a segment in the lapse of the individuals life; a stage of psycho-biological development; an element of social replacement; a stage in life marked by incomplete access to social positions; a marginal social category; a constellation of ideologically homogeneous cohorts etc. S.N. Eisenstadt, however, seeks more specifically sociological criteria. In his book *Archetypical Patterns of Youth* (1962), Eisenstadt defines youth as a "period of transition from childhood to full adult status of full membership in society. In this period, the individual is no longer a child especially from a physical and sexual point of view but is ready to undertake many attributes of an adult and to fulfil the adult roles. But he is not acknowledged as an adult, a full member of society. Rather he is being 'prepared' or is preparing himself for such adulthood". This definition stresses the place of youth in society as a member yet not a full member of society. Further Eisenstadt looks upon youth as a transition stage. Just as infancy gives way to childhood, youth gives way to adulthood but one step before it. This view is typically sociological in that it stresses that youth should be seen as both a product of social reproduction and a force for social change. These two roles: social reproduction and social change/ transformation could be pursued as a result of the young people in question differentiating between what they accept and what they wish to change in a given social setup or by replicating patterns of older generation or pursuing a path of social transformation by participating in movements for social change.

In contemporary societies, we have witnessed many such types of movements by youth. Examples can be what we witnessed in the late 1960's, marked by the rise of *hippies*, who in the west represented the nonviolent protestation of the youth over Western values. They want to be left alone to do their thing—to do what they like for as long as they like without the constraints of the mores and laws of the civilization in which they have grown up. Equally closer to 1970's we witnessed the movements of the underprivileged seeking redress for personally felt social disabilities. The Black Panthers of America among Negroes inspired the similar militant movements elsewhere—such as Dalit Panthers among the suppressed and the backward castes in India. Further instances of revolutionary agitation can be illustrated by the youth agitation in China in 1987. In India specifically 1970 onwards number of youth agitations may be cited like the anti-reservation agitation in Gujarat in 1985, the All Assam Students Union agitation in Assam in 1984, the anti-Mandal agitation in north India in 1990. Moreover youth played a part in the militant's agitation for Khalistan in Punjab and for an independent Kashmir in Jammu and Kashmir.

Though functional in their own way, all these agitations and protests had some tragic consequences like increasing disorder, mass killing, a reign of terror, smuggling of weapons, criminalization of politics etc. Nevertheless from this backdrop, Indian youth seem sensible, sensitive, and politically conscious, and have a reasonable amount of disillusion with the political class. It is something so obvious in some contemporary surveys that across the major cities and towns of India very huge numbers of young people criticizes dynastic politics and prefer that people with criminal records should not be allowed to contest elections. While a considerable chunk of them want uniform civil code, they are also against religion processions (see *India Today,* Feb. 20, 2006:12-57; DeSouza, *et al.,* 2009). Hence, there seems to be a readiness for religious reforms and a growing attitude towards secularism. Using the well known Marxian concept, it could be stated that important historical events in India have to some extent contributed to the transformation of youth from a social category "in itself" into a category "for itself" into a social group conscious of its peculiar social conditions, its aspirations and ideology.

However, this is not the only facet that pertains to the contemporary Indian youth, rather their dissatisfaction with an established social order, expression in trendy dress patterns and non-conformist ideas, art forms and style of life also arrests the attention of social scientists in general and sociologists in particular. Scholars, who have written on Indian youth generally, argue that youth are taking up less responsibility and obligation towards living with old and have expressed problems with aged due to their way of living and behaviour, reflecting the weakness in family structure. For example according to Royse and Verghese's (2007: 33-36) study conducted in the urban areas of Kerala, 82 percent boys and 92 percent girls between the age group of 21-30 years, criticized over the negative feelings, the elders have over the modern dress worn by youth. The study also reveals that nearly 50 percent of youth were not happy to spend time with elders as it always ended in clash, because interest in pleasure is stronger for majority of youth than interest in more serious activities. Sex and violence seem to have become two of the major television themes, which offer new examples of behaviour to youth, and which they tend to practice in real life. As per the report published in *The Week/ Cvoter* (2007:32-43), 46 percent respondents between the age-group of 15-19 years of the total sample of 1004, across ten cities of India feel that sex is just for fun. While 61 percent don't regret losing their virginity, 22 percent said to have done so by class 12th. Social scientists, who study social trends, point to a rise in premarital sex in urban and rural areas. The population council 2006-2007 survey of Maharashtra shows that nearly 14 percent of urban males have had premarital sex, the figures being 25 percent for rural male, the corresponding figures for females are 11 percent and 23 percent of urban and rural areas respectively.

The change is more in the outlook towards these relationships, which consequently has led to the sharp rise in the transmission of HIV/ aids infection. Globally almost one fourth 1/4 of those living with Aids are under the age of 25 years (discussed later in the chapter). Particularly in India one fourth (1/4) of the total estimated 5 million people infected with HIV/ Aids are in the 15-24 age group (UN, 2005).

Besides there is vulnerability of young people to many other risky behaviours such as excessive alcohol consumption, drug abuse and attempted suicide etc. There is an estimated one billion smokers including heavy drug takers in the world today. Especially in the Central Asia and Eastern Europe up to 25 percent of those who inject drugs are estimated to be less than 20 years of age (World Bank 2007). Talking about India, the drug abuse and alcohol consumption is not prevalent in male youth only, the economic independence and changed social environment helped break down of middle class taboos against women drinking and gave emergence to new issues. Women drinkers between the 15-25 age group account for a quarter of the Indian alcohol industries annual 15 percent growth (*Out Look,* 2008: 51-64).

Putting all the pieces together, the broad based empirical generalizations of foregoing enable us to maintain that youth including Indian youth in the current generation come across as both individualistic fun-seekers and frail pragmatists, and we would argue, these are the two sides of same coin. Being fun-seekers, it is probably in many cases youth, who are irrational and undisciplined. However and therefore every country needs to pay a great deal of attention to this segment of population, particularly India, which is predominately very young as 38.8 percent population is between the 10-29 year age group. Because progress of a society depends upon the utilization of youth potential; as Karl Mannheim in his *Diagnosis of Our Times* (1943: 3-6), put forward that, "dynamic societies will rely mainly upon the cooperation of youth." Therefore, this means that ill or good effects on youth are likely to have a long term consequences.

Youth in the International Discourse

The historical and theoretical background of sociological literature on youth can be well traced at least as far back as Auguste Comte's *Positive Philosophy*. In the fourth volume of *Positive Philosophy Lecture 51,* he put forward a hypothesis according to which the rate of change in society was related to the succession of generations: "The shorter the life-span of a generation, the more forceful the social change" (Kuczynski *et al.* 1988: 3).

This hypothesis was disproved by the course of social and demographic developments in twentieth century. It may however, be regarded as the first important contribution to the sociology/ sociological theory of youth. This hypothesis makes it clear that youth is a factor of social change: not because it is subjected to the socializing influence of the adult institutions and a stage in formation of social identity. Moreover, youth is an important element in the process of historical development and of cultural change/ transformation. Auguste Comte was contended that youth is endowed with the "instincts of change". And as a positivist his ideal of progress was related to the positive evaluation of youth and opposed the tradition—oriented conservative forces. But at the same time, he was very much critical of the disruptions of social order.

Specifically at the beginning of the twentieth century, G.S Hall's theory of personality development started a trend of psychological and socio-psychological studies focused on adolescence as a special subject of research. He introduced this new term adolescence in his book *On Adolescence* (1904). His main arguments, however, were culture bonded, class bonded and philosophical rather than scientific, and are representing the reflections of evolutionary theorists.

Although individual historical, literary or ethnological studies of youth culture phenomena were conducted early on with a certain amount of parallel discussions from a psychoanalytical vantage point, it was in the 1960's that a more comprehensive and diversified treatment of youth cultural forms and activities appear and was developed in several countries (Forans and Bolin, 1995: 5-6). J.S Coleman's research report in his book *Adolescent Society* (1961) was in some way considered comprehensive research report limited to one problem and based on one questionnaire. Because of the vast array of research techniques used in this research, it was for a long time considered most remarkable approach in western sociological literature on youth and adolescents.

Nonetheless in the Worlds Tenth Congress of Sociology (1982) in Mexico, there had been a presentation of documents regarding youth movements, wherein youth was held as the *nineteen sixties global generation.* However, this statement was not applicable world-wide because, there were still differences in the life conditions of young people in different parts of the world. And such differences were brought out in the same congress about the Indian village youth and Japanese youth from vocational orientation centre and about frustrated Moroccan boys in Dutch cities. Besides this, in a paper from UNESCO various differences in the context of Asia were alone presented on the mobilization of Asian youth for social activity and development.

The international youth year (1985) was an attempt to end these differences and fragmentation in identifying, conceptualizing and attempting solutions to the specific problems of young people worldwide. Consequently the concept of youth became very much a part of international discourse and the international development strategy for the Third United Nations Development Decade recommended that all countries should give priority to the mobilization and integration of youth in development, which in turn sharpened the designation of (1985) as international youth year.

That said, in reality the differences in the situation and conditions of youth in different parts of the world still exist. The best illustration in this respect would be Brown *et al.* (2002) *The Worlds Youth: Adolescence in Eight Regions of the Globe.* This study in its totality is a remarkable an attempt by an international team of scholars to comment on the youth of eight regions of the world. To begin with, this scholarly piece reveals that there is absorption, assimilation and influence coming from the globalization process, but not uniformization. The more the world globalizes, the more gaps between countries or regions increase; inequalities are becoming apparent within societies as well. People speak of the emergence of a *global youth culture* and view that youth wear the same clothing and hair style, listen to some of the same music, share same challenges, interest and concerns, but in reality differences of the situations of youth and of the frames that contribute to the shaping of their lives remain strengthened. In Arab societies for instance, strong traditional system of family relationship is operating, religion is strong and governs the actions and behaviour of young people. Obedience to fathers and elders is almost unquestionable. Similarly in China and Japan, there are strong family centered traditions and family honour remains crucial motivation to young people in their educational and carrier choices etc. Whereas in the Western and European countries, greater openness and weakening authority of parents may contribute to the relatively higher rates of deviant behaviour that characterize several North American societies as well. Similarly these societies display differences in their response to the role of peer groups in socialization and development of the youth. Opportunities for peer interactions are severely limited in Arab States, especially for girls. Where as in Africa, North America and Europe, peer groups play like substitute families. Indeed in this backdrop it could be held that the increased rates of sexual activity among South Asian youth is casually related to decreased parental supervision resulting from mother's employment and young people's migration to cities for employment (Maria, 2002: 171-206). Equally in terms of gender the societies such as Indian, Latin American, Southeast Asian and Arab display a toleration gape when it comes to sexual adventures among boys, but in same societies opportunities for girls to develop romantic and sexual relations are highly restricted.

Thus all these situations and conditions of youth lives, identified, evaluated and discussed by various scholars from different regions of the world prevents us from considering that there is a single new generation, rather this generation is made of worlds that have almost nothing to share. And hence one must look closely to identify the challenges that young people face in twenty first century. In fact looking through the lens of broader global perspective, we are living in a very young world, indeed, with roughly half of the current global population under the age of 25 (World Bank, 2007). Nonetheless, given the socio-economic terrain of the world youth upon closer inspection, it is possible to sketch out four broad analytic categories of young people. The first category is an increasingly thin upper stratum of young people, generally men, who acquire high quality education in elite institutions and step easily into secure salaried employment, often within the professions or business. The second category comprises of young people who are by and large engaged in paid employment. For example, in the global South, according to International Labour Organisation (ILO) statistics for the year 2008, nearly 35 percent of women and 59 percent of men aged between 15 to 19 years are engaged in paid employment[2] (see also Reynolds 1991, Miles 1998, Dyson 2006, 2008). The third category is a very large section of the remaining youth, partly or wholly engaged in unpaid agricultural or domestic labour, and in certain cases many of these young people, especially from rural peasants and urban poor families,

---

[2]   See http://www.prb.org [accessed 13 June 2011].

work in harsh, hazardous, or abusive conditions (Shanahan *et al.* 2002). In this area of concern, the youth of the former Soviet Union (FSU) societies cannot be lost sight of. Therefore, a fourth category is analytically drawn to represent those young people, though they fit in first three categories, who saw their world turned upside down. Certainly, with the Soviet Union disintegrated many Central Asian young people, who were once valorised as the Great State of the Future and brought up in an environment that shaped them according to the so-called Moral Code of Communism (Kuehnast, 2000), found their status reduced and their financial and political future uncertain. Once these young people enjoyed easy access to education, a near-100 percent literacy rate, full employment, and a reliable and free medical system (ICG, 2003: 1); preschools, kindergartens, children's sanitariums, milk kitchens (a Soviet shop where milk was given free to children), summer camps, and after-school facilities were provided:

The younger generation that is coming of age in Central Asia today is a group that finds itself worlds apart from its Soviet-raised parents, and it bears the stamp of this unique and difficult transition. In less than a decade, the countries have politically, economically, and socially reconstituted themselves. Although remnants of Soviet-era values remain entrenched among their parents' generation, the younger cohort is caught, in many ways, between two worlds. These young people know little about the once-highly centralized and socialized economy, and they have even less comprehension of how their newly decentralized governments and often corrupted new economies can offer any sort of future security for them. Yet they do recognize their own vulnerability and the vulnerability of their young Central Asian states. (Kuehnast 2000: 198)

A majority of young people have become dispossessed of their right to education, work, and culture. While a tiny elite youth immersed in conspicuous consumption have monopolised places in universities and decent jobs, the dispossessed majority are struck by despair and poverty. These emerging inequalities have become much wider and deeper than those of peasantry and artisans under the stage of primitive accumulation of capital (Rigi 2003: 35-6).

In a nutshell, young Central Asians, who were seen in the Soviet setting as undifferentiated and generally an unthinking mass that required close supervision and guidance to ensure ideological loyalty, are now barely thought of by policymakers. Today young people in this region have higher rates of unemployment, poor health, and drug use and are more likely to be victims of violence. Speaking generally, the unemployment rate in this region has reached double-digit numbers. Almost one out of every three, i.e. 33 percent, young people aged 15-25 are unemployed in Central Asia (US Census Bureau, 2005).[3] In fact O'Higgins (2010: 32-3) observes the average youth unemployment and jobless rates still ranging from 26 percent to 28 percent for Central Asian countries.

---

[3] Figures are from United States Census Bureau. 2005. Available at: http://www.census.gov/ipc/www/idb sum.htm [accessed 25 March 2011].

Because this region witnessed an increasing unemployment, the surveys of young people in Eastern Europe and Central Asia, carried out for the World Bank's World Development Report 2007, suggest that access to jobs, along with physical security, are young people's utmost concerns. Currently there are around 22.3 million young people in Eastern Europe and Central Asia living on less than US$1 or 2 a day, and about 27 percent of young people aged 15-24 are neither in school nor employed (United Nations, 2005: 32). Such a magnitude of unemployment and poverty has many socially disruptive repercussions. For example, consistent with the UNAids Report 2008, HIV prevalence in Central Asia and Eastern Europe has escalated by 66 percent since 2001, bringing the number of people living with HIV to 1.5 million, and making it the only region where HIV prevalence clearly remains on the rise. The epidemic here is concentrated more among people who inject drugs and among sex workers (half a million injecting drug users and 80 percent of sex workers in Central Asia and Commonwealth Independent States (CIS) respectively are under the age of 25 years) (UNAIDS 2008).

Gauging the experiences of young people from this broader global perspective, it is clear that marked variabilities in social contexts create deep fissures in the experiences of youth from one nation to another, or among different economic or social groups within a nation. Within societies the worries of youth from economically deprived backgrounds contrast sharply with the optimism of their age mates from economically advantaged circumstances. The underlying theme of the present book pertains to this backdrop, wherein we shall be addressing the broad current sociological discussions both theoretical (individualisation thesis) and empirical (global uniformization thesis) with a grounded approach (see chapter 3rd and 4th). In what follows we shall be pondering over some of the clear and loud implications vis—a`-vis researching the Indian youth.

Indian Youth: Categories in Transition

As gauged in the aforementioned, the emergence of youth as a major force in national movements in various parts of the world is a significant phenomenon of the twentieth century. No less important was the role of youth in the freedom movements particularly in Asia. In India a large number of young men and women were actively involved in the freedom struggle under Gandhi's leadership. However, it is only in post independence period which is marked by an increasing focus of academic studies and research works on youth with an increasing recognition of the existence of youth and youth culture as distinct and separate entity from adult society. There has been considerable attempt by social scientists to empirically identify the different aspects, conditions and problems concerning Indian youth with special reference to their educational and occupational aspirations, their values and attitudes, culture and subculture etc. In order to better understand the scenario of young people, living in the margins of the *local* and the *national* come to be perceived as agents of social change and researching them has become a growth industry among social scientists working in widely ranging settings.

Indeed it is even more explicable and moderately reasonable that researching young people today are imperative. They are in the forefront of contemporary processes of change, constitute a big chunk of not only Indian, but world population at large, and are future adults and leaders. According to the *World Development Report* (World Bank, 2007) there are currently 1.5 billion youth between the ages of 12—24 world-wide, 1.3 billion of whom live in developing countries—the most ever in history. With over 200 million youth living in poverty, 130 million illiterate, 88 million unemployed, and 10 million living with HIV/Aids. Not surprisingly the largest proportion of youth living in poverty can be found in South Asia, which accounts for four out of every ten young people living on less than US$ one or two a day (UN 2005). Therefore, on the whole the cases for investing in young people today are clear and loud.

Exclusively in a country, being second populous in the world with great socio—cultural diversity like India where about 4,635 communities (Singh 1992) co-exist and where religion, caste, tribe, rural—urban location, gender and currently in certain cases class (Yedla 1992) constitute the important variables, which in combination make for the diversity in the lived experiences of young people, sociology of youth has a wide scope and significance (Jayaram 2000). Additionally the current demographic facts in India like age structure transition and the predictions thereon, also call for the rigorous and inclusive sociological investigations of youth, of their school to work transitions and culture etc. (Jayaram, 2009). If we are to believe the current estimates by demographers and economists, India is and will remain for some time one of the youngest countries in the world.

Table 1.1
Projected Proportion of Youth in Some Selected Countries of the World

Country/Year	2000	2005	2010	2015	2020
India	34.6	34.8	34.8	34.9	34.4
China	34.4	32.4	29.9	29.3	28.5
Brazil	36.5	35.9	34.5	32.4	30.5
US	27.5	27.3	27.2	26.5	25.7
Germany	26.2	23.8	22.9	22.4	21.4

Source: *World Bank, URL: http://devdata.worldbank.org/hnpstats/dp1.asp*
Note: *Figures pertain to age group 15—34 years.*

These projections can have both positive as well as negative implications for India and therefore, warrants urgent social scientists and policy maker's attention. The availability of a human resource of such magnitude for achieving socio—economic change and technological excellence needs commensurate infrastructure and suitable priorities to maximize its contribution to national development. For the reason that it is the quality of young people that will decide the level to which India can reap this "demographic gift" that too in a shorter period of time,[4] it requires good amount of human resource investment in youth. As Shariff (2007: 12) demonstrates that "India's disadvantage is its unskilled, uneducated workforce which could undermine its global competitive strengths and expose the economy to the risk of stagnation. The growing mismatch between the nature of educated manpower and the demands of newly established companies will pose a serious challenge within the next decade".

Given these issues, there is an urgent need to map the orientations, aspirations, apprehensions and constraints and anxieties of young people across the country, keeping in consideration each and every section, and therefore give young people equal opportunities, while remaining with the broader framework of national and regional cultures, and the present changing social scenario.

The literature on the Indian youth, that we have been referring in the aforementioned, cast youth as "student" (Ahluwalia 1972: 3) and one is likely to come across flood of literature on student youth when reading upon Indian youth (e.g. Shah 1964, Fuer 1969, Sarkar 1974, Lakshminarayana 1985). It is likely that student youth during the time this literature come about was urban youth, because in 1960s, 70s till 80s rural youth were far behind in terms of education and majority of students all over the country were urban youth.

---

[4] As it is clear in table 1.1 that the percentage of the 15-34 age tappers off from 2020 onwards, there will be increases in dependent population i.e. 60 plus.

Therefore it is understandable that rural youth, the majority of Indian youth population and non student youth have received a scant attention all over and unfair so, is the case with tribal youth. Although some scholars have carried a little, that is however, cursory treatment, rather than full analysis. Even currently more focus (e.g. Rampal 1999, Joshi 2003, Babar, and Perry *et al.,* 2010) is being paid on urban and metropolitan youth to the neglect of the emerging small town, rural and tribal youth which constitute a big portion of youth population in India and there is practically nothing worthy to mention the studies on tribal youth. Let's look at the statistical analysis of Indian youth.

Table 1.2
Indian Youth by Age, Location and Caste/ Tribe

	Of Total Population	Of Youth Population (15-34)
Location:		
Rural	72.2	69.5
Urban	27.8	30.8
Caste/Tribe:		
Scheduled Caste	16.6	15.9
Scheduled Tribe	8.4	7.9

Source: *Census of India, 2011, Office of Registrar General, Government of India.*

Table 1.3

Indian Youth by Levels of Education, Location, Caste and Tribe

	Literacy Rate	Below Primary	Primary	Middle	Secondary	Hr. Secondary	Graduate & above
Location:							
Rural	65.4	8.7	16.8	15.6	13.7	6.7	3.9
Urban	84.7	5.6	14.8	16.9	20.8	13.7	12.7
SC/ST:							
SC	60.9	8.6	16.7	14.9	10.8	5.6	2.9
ST	51.8	10.5	13.7	11.4	8.3	3.8	1.9

Source: *Census of India, 2011, Office of Registrar General, Government of India.*
Note: *All figures in the table are in percent, indicating the proportion of population in each segment of population.*

Some existing literature classifies Indian youth into two broad categories: (a) tribal, rural and lower-caste youth and (b) middle class and upper middle class youth (Yedla 1992). Here on the basis of above analysis (table 1.2), it is then confirmed that vast majority of Indian youth fall into the first category (see table 1.3) and indicates the educational status of these youth which is comparatively low, and therefore, have to be prepared rightly if India is to fully exploit the demographic gift. But unfortunately most research on Indian youth and their movement focus their attention on second category. It is surprising that on reviewing the literature, we didn't come across any significant studies on tribal youth particularly in the context of Jammu and Kashmir.

The reasons for this lack of literature and information on tribal youth are obvious and understandable: urban student youth are more visible to the media, more vocal when being interviewed and easier to be surveyed. More importantly spend much more on commodities beyond daily necessities and are more open to fashion trends. In short they are better consumers. But this market driven emphasis on young urban consumers has obscured our understanding of Indian youth as a whole. It is evident from national youth policy 2003, which holds that Youth development efforts in India have been hampered by lack of adequate information and research base. The Policy, therefore, suggests the establishment of a well organized Information and Research Network with regard to various areas of concern to the youth to facilitate the formulation of focused youth development schemes and programmes. The policy accorded top priority to rural, tribal and out school youth (Gupta and Gupta 2006).

Thus, it is time to realise that tribal youth are equally important, they constitute a good chunk of youth population in India and they too may have essentially the same kind of aspirations as their counterparts elsewhere in the country. However, their joys and pains, losses and gains, love and hatred rarely enter the sight of scholars. It is in the context of the paucity of studies on tribal youth that we undertook a research study of the youth in Ladakh where about 91.04 percent population are scheduled tribes (Census 2011). This book makes a modest contribution in this area, and is first of its kind in Ladakh in which our effort was to study, understand and explore the changing attitudes and aspirations among youth in spheres of education, occupation, attitude, and interests etc. We begin with a brief profile of the changing scenario in Ladakh, before illustrating what we observed among youth in Ladakh (see chapter 2nd).

Ladakh: A Changing Scenario

Ladakh, the northernmost tip of the India, nestled in the trans—Himalayan region of Kashmir, often referred to as *Little Tibet*, is a semi-autonomous region in the Indian State of Jammu and Kashmir. Geographically situated on the western extension of the Tibetan plateau, Ladakh has cultural and linguistic affinities with Tibet of China (Rizvi 1996). There is a mystical quality about Ladakh that lends it—self generously to the creative urges of travel writers and research scholars alike *Moon Land; the Last Shangri-la* and *Forbidden Himalayan Kingdom* are the some other phrases that one is likely to come—across when reading upon this region. The Ladakhi culture (it should be mentioned, is an amorphous construct at best {Martjin 2003}) has been praised for the successful and self-sufficient methods with which it has survived centuries.

However, Ladakh today doesn't offer the similar case. Like many beautiful, self-sufficient regions in the world, Ladakh has been impacted by external forces and caused massive and rapid transformations. At the core of this phenomenon are the ongoing process of modernisation and the linkage of a traditional subsistence economy to regional and national markets (Michaud 1996). Globalization as well has taken all forms in Ladakh. From intervention by the World Bank and IMF to tourist—driven cultural reforms, Ladakh is changing. As in many mountain areas, Ladakh is now a typical example of an "internal periphery" (Michaud 1996: 286-87), whose destiny is largely controlled by a Centralized, lowland political power (Skeldon 1985, Ives and Messerli 1989).

Every year thousands of tourists from Europe, Japan and U.S.A etc., visit Ladakh, and there must hardly be a corner of this land that has not been thoroughly explored and documented by eager adventurers. For instance during the year 2006-07, the department of tourism has registered 43821 tourists of whom 17707 were Indian and 16114 were foreigners, the number is expected to increase (District Statistics and Evaluation Agency 2007: 26-27). Therefore, it is tourism; more than any other economic sector, through that Ladakh earns millions of rupees every year and has raised the standard of living and purchasing power of the local inhabitants. Today one can see hotels, guest houses, restaurants and travel agencies as a good source of employment. Moreover, tourism helps increase the scope of employment by encouraging entrepreneurship in handicraft industry, painting, clay arts etc. Western-style medicine, government subsidy of farmers, more imports, population rising and Ladakhis' moving to city, because of the economy are other indications of modernization in Ladakh.

Resultantly in Leh, urbanisation at the level of 25.37 percent is similar to both the State 27.21 percent and national 31.16 percent averages (Census 20011). Particularly in the last two decades, the population of Leh has more than tripled in size (Goodall 2004). For a more detailed discussion of contemporary change and development in Ladakh see Norberg-Hodge (1991) and Rizvi (1996, 1999).

Research Design and Methodology

The prime bearing of the above mentioned that create a centre of our attention, is the increase in the cultural disorganization and increase in the individualization which allows a great freedom of action and choice to the individual. And replacement of single social fabric of meanings emblematic of Ladakhi community in which same kind of people were doing same kind of things by that of the numerous goals, actions and meanings of modern urban life which in a sense resulted into the tremendous rise in the level of aspirations. By and large it is the youth who have been in the forefront in this quest for differentiation and individualism. Some of the common impacts of this erosion particularly on younger generation are visible to layman, because youth, who work as tourist guides earn easy money and get exposed to western culture, does reflect in their day-to-day life, be it their dress or food habits etc. Thus with the march of glitzy and attractively packaged life style of the outside world Ladakhi youth prefer to dress, talk and live like foreigners, developing a subtle contempt for their own culture in the process. At the superficial level, some of the main items/ customs which are seen declining from the Ladakhi culture are:

- ☐ *Esun:*—A type of dance by the young and old during gathering or at picnic time or festivals is rarely seen in during the present-day occasions, disco dances and western music has taken its place instead (Vidhya, 2006: 111-115).

☐ *Chospuns:*—A type of relationship between young boys and girls, which was previously based on the advice of the prominent lama's of the area, is now generally depending up to the individual boys' and girls' wishes and is not on the constructive footings at present. Though *chospuns* do exist but their role is nominal.

☐ *Phasphun:*—Another type of important relationship depicting good culture was Phusphun. This relationship would exist between neighbouring families for volunteer-services on important ceremonies like marriage, birth-ceremonies and funeral ceremonies. These families have to present themselves on all these occasions for volunteer services irrespective of any kinship relations with parties, however because of the busy schedule of the working class people this custom is also seen at its decreasing trend (Singh, 1994: 189-191).

Against this backdrop and given the viability of access, we located our field work in Leh of Ladakh which is the nerve Centre and one of the most widely travelled province in Ladakh. It is the major administrative, commercial and tourist centre of Ladakh. Apart from tourism, due to the implementation of developmental programmes by Central government, globalization of culture, marketization of economy and mass media etc. as mentioned above, Leh is representing a continuous process of social change indicating distinct points of urban development. At present, with the population of 133487 and a shocking sex ratio of just 690, which is a massive drop of 133 from the 2001 census figures, Leh is representing a cosmopolitan crowd of Ladakhis, Tibetans, Kashmiris, and people from other States of India, all stay together in harmony adhering different religions. However, it is Buddhism which dominates the scene in and around the Leh. Talking about the modern macro level developments, the area coming under the domain of Leh notified area committee (NAC), there is one government degree college, one polytechnic college, one ITI centre, three higher secondary schools, nine high schools and sixty nine other institutions in whole Leh block run by State government and three reputed educational institutions run by the Central government namely Central Institute of Buddhist Studies Choglamsar (CIBS), Kendra Vidhyalaya Leh (K.V), and Jawahar Navodhya Vidhayalaya Leh (J.N.V). Specifically in the Leh town, there is one cinema hall and one auditorium hall with the seating capacity of 430 and 200 respectively.

Besides, in order to raise the socio-economic conditions of the people of region, recently the National Informatics Centre (NIC) of information and technology ministry has setup six Community Information Centres (CIC) in all blocks of Leh district viz; Leh, Kharu and Nubra etc., to help the people to avail the benefits of global connectivity through internet. Hence people of the region particularly youth got much exposed to the outside world, which in sense fascinated them. With this understanding an attempt was made to locate youth both male and female between the age group of 15-25 years of Leh, which comprises the universe of the study, and their sub-culture in relation to rest of society from which to identify what may be distinctive about contemporary youth in Ladakh, in spheres of education, occupation, attitude and interests etc. Specifically the objectives of the study which was carried out during May-July 2010 in Leh included as follows:

- ☐ To determine the personal and socio-economic characteristics of youth under reference to ascertain how far the differential location in social structure determines variation in the lives of youth.
- ☐ To know how far the modern values such as achievement orientation and social mobility are being developed among youth with special reference to educational orientations and occupational aspirations.
- ☐ To indicate their time-use pattern to reflect upon their dominant interests and leisure time activity.
- ☐ To know what special interests are associated in their approach to mass media, dress pattern, food habits and mixing with opposite sex?

Operationalization of the Concepts Used

Youth: The literature review of many youth programmes indicates that the concept youth lacks a universally accepted definition because of variation in the age at which physical maturation takes place in different geo-cultural conditions. However, a careful assessment of such programmes show attempts to define youth into exclusive categories such as school children, un-married school leavers, those who have out-grown infancy but are dependent on parents or guardians, those under eighteen years of age and above ten years, urban youth, farm youth etc. According to United Nations, the term youth is used to indicate young men and women between the age group of fourteen and twenty five years. Some existing national youth services use sixteen to thirty-two years of age group. In Indian context the seventh five year plans opening paragraphs on the census gives us an idea that youth is between 15-35 years of age for planning considerations. The encyclopaedia of social work in India limits youth to 16-24 years age group. However, for the sake of practical convenience the youth for present study would mean all men and women in the age of 15-25 years. As an attempt has been made in this study to cover both educational and occupational youth, this definition is not only statistical in nature but sociological as well.

Youth Culture: Kroeber and Kluckholn (1952: 2) synthesized a definition of culture based on an analysis of one hundred and sixty (160) definitions drawn from different social sciences. They conclude: "Culture consists of patterns, explicit and implicit of symbols, constituting the distinctive achievements of human groups, including their embodiments in artefacts; the essential core of culture consists of traditional (i.e. historically derived and selected) ideas and especially their attached values; culture systems may on the one hand, be considered as products of action, and on the other as conditioning elements of further action."

However for the purpose of the present study youth culture may be defined as those characteristic attitudes, interests and practices that young people bring into play in meeting their social, psychological, educational and leisure time needs in a given social situation.

Sample and Sampling Technique

The actual number of respondents included in the sample was 150 (comprising of 90 male and 60 female youth). The less representation to female was based on census records which shows Leh block having lowest sex ratio i.e. 730 female per thousand male, in Jammu and Kashmir. Further, the sample was assumed to give representation to organized/ unorganized occupational and educational youth groups living in Leh. So to keep the methodological consistency of the study, 38 respondents i.e. 25.33 percent out of the total said sample has been drawn from occupational youth groups and the rest of 112 respondents i.e. 74.66 percent of sample have been drawn from educational youth groups.

The primary reasons for selecting majority of student youth was high literacy rate i.e. more than 80 percent of the area coming under the domain of Leh notified area committee, which became one of the important factor for sampling. Therefore it was felt that student youth would be in majority in the town.

The selection criteria for the respondents on the basis of "quota sampling" has been a male or female, married or unmarried, working or non working, student or non student but between the age group of 15-25 years and living in Leh. The reasons for adopting quota sampling technique have been that of incomplete sampling frames and non response. For the population of young people between the age group of 15-25 years in Leh, school and college rolls might had constituted a sampling frames, but that would have excluded youth living in the area being schooled out of area, and included youth from other areas being schooled within it, and would have also excluded a minority of working youth in the Leh. Furthermore, since selection is not blind in quota sampling, it relies on the judgment of the interviewer as to who to approach and who to include. Hence there is no non-response in a quota sampling.

Tools Used in Data Collection

Since the study intended to avail of highly personal information from respondents, interview schedule seemed to be the most appropriate tool to be used for data collection. The use of this tool made it possible to encourage, break the ice and build up rapport with the respondents. It also allowed the respondents to ask for clarification and explanation of unclear or difficult questions. Some topics like mixing with opposite sex which is generally not freely discussed and is more so when the interviewer is stranger, to get the relevant and correct information, rapport had to be established to remove obstacles and gain the confidence of respondents.

The interview schedule consisting of seventy six questions was originally drafted in English. However, the schedule was highly structured with the interviewer simply reading and recording the answers based on predetermined alternatives. Additional information based on observations and interviews with people (potential informers), who have had the opportunity of intimate contact with the subjects under study, was noted on a separate notebook.

As stated earlier, the sample included both educational and occupational youth, researcher started data collection with the student youth. For that the permission of the heads of different academic, technical and professional institutions was sought prior to starting of interviews. After introducing himself and the purpose of the research work, heads or (man in charge) of every institution have been co-operative. They allowed researcher to go up to class rooms of their institutions and also each provided an assistant with whose help, researcher could identify easily only those respondents who were at present living in Leh. Similarly with occupational youth, their permission was sought prior to starting of interviews. At the start of an interview, researcher introduced himself and talked in brief about the study. They (respondents) were also told that the information given by them would be kept strictly confidential. But when it came to the topic of sex, there was a little hesitancy on the part of some respondents. They looked down and then at researchers face, may be to see if he himself was comfortable.

The average time for each interview was about thirty minutes to an hour and later on two to three hour each day was spent for writing additional information. Each day at least five to seven interviews would take place. Hence it took researcher about three month to complete data collection.

Data Processing

After the collection of data, first step was the coding. A code list was prepared and the answers filled in the interview schedule were manually coded. Rechecking of coded sheets was done in order to avoid any error. Second step was to prepare the tables for the final analysis of data.

- □ **Simple Frequency and Percentage Tables:** These tables provide the socio-economic background and self interests and aspirations of respondents.
- □ **Bi-variate Tables:** These tables provide the information of aspirations, attitudes and life-style of respondents with reference to various variables like gender, monthly income, family background etc.

Moreover, percentage of responses were calculated out of both, responses in each particular category, say male/ female and student/ non student, and out of the total number of respondents in the study (n = 150).

Encounters and Experiences

On the whole it (data collection) went off well. Yet no research work is smooth sailing. A few obstacles are bound to arise. It depends on how one takes them.

- Firstly problems of communication arise. Many respondents couldn't comprehend terms like, 'materialistic', 'research', 'virginity' etc. even after being interpreted in Urdu by researcher.
- Secondly, a problem of rapport building, particularly between researcher and female respondents came up.
- Thirdly, financial problem arise during study which in turn put constraint on time use pattern.
- Fourthly, the problem of non-response. Since Quota-sampling which researcher adopted, is free from such limitations. Yet it pinches the courage of researcher.
- Fifthly, the problem of photography. Majority of respondents didn't cooperate when it came to click a photograph. Well all this is a part of research, because though valuable to the research work, a respondent had the liberty to say 'No'.
- Lastly, but not of least importance is the problem of permission of the authority. On the whole the heads of all institutions were co-operative except in one case where we were not allowed to carry on his research work.

2

Youth and Social Change in Ladakh

Mostly it is during the restless and mobile period of youth that the need and desire to test the new and carve-out individual identities is strongest. Young people have a great deal of free time and considerable interest in consumption and entertainment (even if the financial means to pursue them is lacking). Therefore, to understand choices of different life-styles or rather the choice of life style—it is necessary to look at the different preconditions and possibilities that young people hold when they choose how they wish to live. Structural factors such as gender, class and religion etc. are important in this perspective, but their significance is not associated with being born into a certain class or religion at a certain time, but consists of what these factors mean today to the extent that these factors are a living part of everyday life (in the same way as one's hopes for the future and probable career affect how one chooses to live today). Moreover, study of structural or background factors like age, parental education, family pattern and family income etc. is useful to understand how one is affected by these processes in different ways.

Now-withstanding, in the present study the constellation of questions have been put to subjects under study to ascertain their age, gender, religion, parental education, family income, family pattern etc. With these background variables certain associations have been made to know how for the differential location in social structure determines variation in the lives of youth.

Age and Gender

Table 2.1 summarizes the age and gender characteristics of the respondents and reveals that of the total one hundred and fifty (150) sample, 52.6 percent belonged to the age group of 16-20 years, while 47.3 percent were in the age group of 21-25 years.

Table 2.1

Age and Gender of Research Participants

Age Years	Gender		
	Male (%)	Female (%)	Total (%)
16-20	47(52.2)	32(53)	79(52.6)
21-25	43(47.7)	28(46.6)	71(47.3)
Total	**90(100)**	**60(100)**	**150(100)**

With respect to gender 52.2 percent male and 53 percent female respondents were in the lower age group, whereas 47.7 percent male and 46.6 percent female respondents were in the upper age group. However, considered as a whole, further analysis indicates that from the total said sample 60 percent were male whereas 40 percent were female youth.

Gender and Religion

Albeit Buddhists are in majority in Leh District, our respondents who reported their religious affiliations were from three religions. Table 2.2 shows that majority (68.6 percent) of respondents were Buddhists, followed by Muslims (30.6 percent). Just one (0.66 percent) respondents were Hindus.

Table 2.2

Gender and Religion of Research Participants

Religion	Male (%)	Female (%)	Total (%)
Buddhism	63(70)	40(66)	103(68.6)
Islam	27(30)	19(31.6)	46(30.6)
Hinduism	—	1(1.66)	1(0.66)
Total	**90(100)**	**60(100)**	**150(100)**

A direct comparison between the distributions of these religious groups in the current sample on the basis of gender reveals that 70 percent male and 66 percent female respondents were Buddhist youth. While, 30 percent male and 31.6 percent female respondents were Muslim youth, and only one i.e., 1.66 percent female respondents out of the total sample were from Hinduism.

Family income

Family income is a major background variable that is supposed to account for variation in the lives of young people. Those belonging to families with high income are likely to have higher living standard compared to those belonging to families with low income. Thus in order to find out percentage of respondents belonging to a particular income group, three income categories: low (below 5000), middle (5000-10000) and high (10000 and above) have been made.

Table 2.3 gives the information on the economic status of the respondents in terms of monthly income of the family. The data here show that 29.3 per cent of the respondents in the sample belonged to low-income category of below Rs.5000 per month. Nearly half (48 percent) of the youth in the study belonged to medium-income category of Rs.5000-10000 per month, whereas only 22.6 per cent belonged to high-income category with a monthly income of over Rs.10000. The analysis of data here reveals that majority (70.6 percent) of respondents were from a class of families with a monthly income of over Rs.5000.

Table 2.3
Youth by their Family Monthly Income
and by Occupational Status

Occupational Status			
Monthly income:	Student (%)	Working/non-student (%)	Total (%)
Low (Below 5000)	27(24.1)	17(44.7)	44(29.4)
Medium (5000-10000)	56(50)	16(42.1)	72(48)
High (10000 & above)	29(28.8)	5(13.15)	34(22.6)
Total	**112(100)**	**38(100)**	**150(100)**

Majority (112 out of 150) of the youth in the study were students and the remaining 38 respondents were working. Analysis of the data on the association between family income and present occupational status of respondents shows that on the whole the family income of the working students was lower than that of the non-working students. While low income group constituted 44.7 per cent of the non-student/ working youth, only 24.1 per cent of the student youth belonged to the low-income category. This indicates that the families of lower income group were not in a position to spare their youth for higher education. Many times, parents with low income desire to engage even their children in some work, while the medium and high income groups which usually consist of relatively better educated parents may not only encourage their children for higher education, but also arrange and invest their resources for the same. Our data further highlight that a very low percentage (13.2 percent) of non-student youth and over one fourth (25.9 percent) of the student youth had a family income of over Rs.10000 per month.

Parental Education

Parent's education is an another background factor that acts as an influencing factor in the personality development and has a profound impact on an individual's values and attitudes, because personality variables-valuation for education, motivation for education and educational aspirations are not independent. For the analytical purposes in the present study, parental education has been categorized into three levels: low (below high school level), medium (higher secondary and under graduate level) and high (graduation and above). Contrary, respondents on their basis of educational level have been classified into: illiterate, primary, middle, secondary and higher secondary and undergraduate.

Table 2.4 presents the educational level achieved by the respondents and their parents. As majority (112 out of 150) of the youth in the sample were students, most (78 percent) of them were educated beyond the middle school level. There were just three illiterate and 13 primary school educated respondents in the sample. Thus on the whole the respondents of the study were youth who had some level of formal education.

Table 2.4
Parental Education and Educational Level
of Research Participants

Educational Level of Respondents						
Parental Education:	Illiterate (%)	Primary (%)	Middle (%)	Sec & Hr. Sec. (%)	Undergraduate (%)	Total (%)
Low	2 (66.6)	9(69.2)	10(58.8)	14(20.5)	12(24.4)	47(31.3)
Medium	1(33.3)	4(30.7)	7(41.1)	35(51.4)	15(30.6)	62(41.3)
High	—	—	—	19(27.9)	22(44.8)	41(27.3)
Total	**3(100)**	**13(100)**	**17(100)**	**68(100)**	**49(100)**	**150(100)**

Further analysis of the data shows that parents of 62 (41.3 percent) respondents were educated up to higher secondary or under-graduation, while parents of 41 (27.3 percent) were at least graduates. On the whole the parents of the youth had more or less the same level of education as their children. It means that the youth of the study were not first generation learners and have had the advantage of some level of educated family background. The data of the study point out to this advantage. All the 41 youth in the sample whose parents were graduates were already educated at least up to the secondary school level. In contrast, nearly half (44.7 percent) of the youth whose parents had education below the level of high school had similarly low level of education. As can be expected, parents with higher level of education would have motivated their children to obtain higher education. Even in the group of youth whose parents had medium level of education (i.e. higher secondary/under-graduation) the vast majority (80.7 percent) were already educated at least up to secondary school level. As our data reveal, youth with secondary and higher secondary levels of education predominantly belonged to parents having medium level of education. This is again indicative of the influence of parental education on their children. Altogether it is suggestive to the fact that low educational level rises as the educational level of parents decrease.

Family Pattern

As a social unit, a family is usually referred to as "a group of persons of both sexes, related by marriage, blood or adoption, performing roles based on age, sex and relationship, and socially distinguished as making up a single household or a sub household." For the practical purpose of the study, family has been classified into three types: nuclear family, joint family and extended family. On the basis of marital status respondents have been classified into two groups: married and unmarried.

Table 2.5
Family Pattern and Marital Status
of Research Participants

	Marital Status		
Family Pattern	Married (%)	Unmarried (%)	Total (%)
Nuclear	2(16.6)	71(51.4)	73(48.6)
Joint	9(75)	67(48.5)	76(50.6)
Extended	1(8.3)	—	1(0.66)
Total	**12(100)**	**138(100)**	**150(100)**

Table 2.5 presents a frequency distribution of respondents according to the type of family they belong and their marital status. Altogether data indicates that 48.62 percent respondents live in nuclear families and 50.6 percent live in joint families, while just a 0.66 percent live in extended families. With respect to marital status the number and percentage of married respondents is higher from joint families whereas only one respondent which constituted 8.33 percent of total married respondents is from extended family. Although respondents are predominantly from joint families, yet the analysis of data reveals a trend in liberalization of attitudes and practices and a change from pre-puberty to post-puberty marriages. Joint families are usually characterized by incidence of child marriage, but that has not been the case here as our data shows that 48.55 percent unmarried respondents are from joint families. Nonetheless, considered as a whole, it is very much discernible from the data presented in above table that majority of youth both from nuclear and joint families now prefer to marry in late twenties or only after the completion of their education or when they have established themselves in life at least from economic point of view.

Perspectives on Education

Social systems and cultures have never been static. Culture is said to be having three components—sociological, ideological and material or economic. At the level of theoretical discussion, the least and the last component exposed to change is the ideological one. The component that gets easily affected in the process of change is material culture followed by social organisation. The Ladakhi society is no exception from this general pattern. Gone are the days when traditional Ladahki society was moulded and shaped by religious beliefs and values, where a very high premium was placed on spirituality. Education was sought with the chief motive of spiritual and philosophical advancements. The most important task of education in general was considered to be promoting society's value over scientific and technical or instrumental rationality. However, this view on education has receded into the background, especially in the recent past, because the exogenous as well as endogenous forces like the increased process of "mediazation," tourism, marketization and implementation of developmental programmes by the Central and State governments in Ladakh have speeded up the modernisation process and established the instrumental rationality in a dominant position in society, which in turn has given rise to the modern materialistic perspectives in the beliefs and ideas of society in general and the young people in particular. Education has come to be regarded as a prerequisite for economic development, and occupational and social mobility.

Table 2.6

Gender and Meaning and Preference of Education

	Gender		
Meaning and preference:	Male (%)	Female (%)	Total (%)
Tech. and professional education	58(64.4)	46(76.6)	104(69.3)
Academic education	9(10)	8(13.3)	17(11.3)
Religious education	11(12.2)	5(8.3)	16(10.6)
All the above	12(13.3)	1(1.6)	13(8.6)
Total	**90(100)**	**60(100)**	**150(100)**

In this changing social scenario young people are looking for organising and re-organising their lives through education, and striving hard for admission in technical and professional colleges. As a result the youth have their own perspective on the goals of education, that reflects the modern western and market driven notion about education. The youth of Lakadh covered in the present study were asked about their views on education, in particular what education means or the type of education they are looking for in the present social situation. Data presented in table 2.6 shows that for majority (69.3 percent) of the youth education today are technical and professional, because it equips one to compete in the modern occupational market and thus provides the opportunities for a decent job. A larger proportion of the student youth, compared to the non-student youth were of this view on education. These courses of education are seen as opening up new vistas of life which enable the educated youth to pursue their aims and plans in life and to make careers for themselves. They consider technical and professional courses more useful, compared to the academic and religious oriented studies. To quote Bourdieu (1986: 249) "when economic capital determines the cultural, symbolic and academic, and human capital; commodification and obsession with money leads to the quantification of all social relations and needs, giving them an exchange value."

Although majority of both male (64.5 percent) and female youth share the above view on education, a larger percentage (76.7 percent) of female respondents view education mainly as technical and professional education and aspire for it. However, in the case of giving holistic view of education, 13.3 per cent of the male respondents included in their view technical, professional, academic and religious education, while only 1.76 per cent of the female respondents expressed this view.

Table 2.7

Gender and Stated Reasons for Giving Preference to Technical and Professional Education

Reasons:	Gender		
	Male (%)	Female (%)	Total (%)
Provides higher govt. job opportunities	31(53.4)	29(63)	60(57)
Trains in skills that are required by economy	17(29.31)	3(6.5)	20(19.2)
Gives high status in Society	7(12.06)	7(15.21)	14(13.4)
Encourages the spirit of competition	3(5.17)	5(10.86)	8(7.69)
All the above	—	2(4.3)	2(1.92)
Total	**58(100)**	**46(100)**	**104(100)**

Thus the data show that female youth too look upon education more as a means for the advancement of one's material position or as a status symbol, rather than as a means for the development of the inner-self. The data also are contrary to the general belief about the view of the traditional and tribal societies, such as Ladakh, on modern education. The notion that the youth in Ladakh have about education reflects the modern attitude based on economic and market demands. And it is perhaps due to this modern attitude towards education and its possibilities that there has been an increase in the number of dropouts amongst younger resident monks/chomos (masculine and feminine forms) in Leh town and its adjoining areas. Moreover, most of those young educated monks/chomos, who get into government departments, turn lay persons, which provides more opportunities for status mobility in the new and modern social hierarchy. Therefore, it can be presumed that the importance which was attached to traditional/religious knowledge is fast diminishing among the Ladakhi youth. It was not the case till the recent past in this religious oriented society; wherein as a practice or religious custom one child was dedicated for religious purposes with all the pride attached to it. The present trend does not seem to be the case anymore. The present crop of youngsters of the Ladakhi society is as materialistic in their outlook as their counterparts elsewhere in the country.

Occupational Aspirations

As already pointed out, modern education inculcates new values that have a vital role in modernising the outlook of the people, and is a significant determinant of social placement. Skill oriented education enables the youth to move from the traditional occupational pursuits to new roles which entail dynamism, achievement orientation, rational means-ends calculations, and new attitudes to wealth, work and risk taking. To some extent, the level of occupational aspiration represents a person's orientation towards achievement of occupational status, which in turn determines one's social status in the sense that occupations, that are functionally more significant and require specialised knowledge and skills, confer higher social status on the incumbent. Nevertheless, certain modern forces, like planned socio-economic changes, modern education, urbanisation, and industrialisation have had their own impact on the occupational aspirations of the youth in particular. New industries, new jobs and new techniques inevitably affect traditional occupations and create new ones.

Table 2.8
Youth by Job Preferences

Nature of Job:	Male (%)	Female (%)	Total (%)
		Gender	
Government	26(28.8)	31(51.6)	57(38)
Business	47(52.2)	21(35.8)	68(45.3)
Private sector	7(7.7)	5(8.3)	12(8)
Traditional parental occupation	3(3.3)	—	3(2)
Agriculture	7(7.7)	3(5)	10(6.6)
Total	**90(100)**	**60(100)**	**150(100)**

The occupational aspirations of the Ladakhi youth have been analysed with reference to five occupational categories, viz. government job, private business, private sector employment, traditional parental occupation and agriculture. Table 2.8 shows that less than half (45.3 percent) of the youth in the sample preferred business. The second preferred job was in the government sector; 38 per cent of the youth in the sample expressed their interest in government jobs. These two categories—business and government job—were preferred by the vast majority (88.3 percent) of the youth. Just three of the respondents (all men) preferred to continue the traditional-parental occupation. The most preferred category among women is that of government jobs. They may be motivated by the fact that many Ladakhi women have already got into lower level government services, probably due to the encouragement from the Ladakh Autonomous Hill

Development Council. The council has thrown open its door to women by reserving seats for them.

Table 2.9

Youth by Occupational Preferences and by Present Occupational Status

Occupational Preferences:	Present Occupational Status		
	Student (%)	Non-Student/ Working (%)	Total (%)
Government	47(41.9)	10(26.3)	57(38)
Business	55(49.1)	13(34.2)	68(45.3)
Private sector job	5(4.46)	7(18.4)	12(8)
Traditional parental occupation	1(0.89)	2(5.2)	3(2)
Agriculture	4(3.57)	6(15.7)	10(6.6)
Total	**112(100)**	**38(100)**	**150(100)**

The data in table 2.9 indicates that a larger percentage (91 percent) of the student youth, compared to the non-student youth (65.5 percent), have shown favourable attitude towards government jobs and business. But in the case of traditional parental occupations, a larger percentage (18.4 percent) of non-student youth than students (4.5 percent) has shown the preference.

The readiness of a relatively large number of youth to take up business as their choice of occupation is understandable in the present social scenario where public sector jobs are very few and competition is ever increasing. However, the case is to some extent different in Ladakh, particularly in Leh, where the onset of market economy and tourism has witnessed a massive growth in trade and commercial activities. And under the circumstances of pragmatic and materialistic considerations, business may prove to be the best offer to the youth.

Table 2.10
Stated Reasons for Giving Preference to Business

	Occupational Status		
	Student	Non-Student/	Total
Reasons:	(%)	Working (%)	(%)
Hereditary	8(14.5)	3(23)	11(16.1)
Enables to earn more money	41(74.5)	9(69.2)	50(73.5)
Gives personal satisfaction	6(10.9)	1(7.6)	7(10.29)
Total	**55(100)**	**13(100)**	**68(100)**

Regarding the reasons, which the respondents have given for preferring business, earning more money, was given by as many as 50 out of the 68 youth who preferred business. It may be noted from further analysis of the data that 11 out of the 68 respondents who opted for business did so, because it was their hereditary occupation. Since Ladakh has been a meeting place of the routes to Tibet in the East, Central Asia in the North, Baltistan in the West, and Kashmir and Punjab in the South, traders and merchants have been coming and going to these places through Ladakh. Leh district in particular was a hub of commercial and trade activities. So, one would expect business as a hereditary occupation in such an area. However, on the whole it may be inferred from the analysis of the data that, among a vast majority of the youth today, work and occupation have assumed economic rather than social and psychological significance. Their view on work and occupation seems to be centred on maximisation of individual material interests that will help them have a comfortable life.

Occupational Mobility

Ideologies based on economic rationalism and monetisation of economy have resulted in occupational diversification, occupational mobility and spatial mobility. It is revealed in the data of the present study of youth in Ladakh that the occupational aspirations of a majority of youth are indicative of generational occupational mobility. Very few respondents think of following their parents' occupation.

Table 2.11
Youth by Occupations Preferred and by Parental Occupation

Occupation Preferred:	Parental Occupation			
	Daily Labourer/ Private Employee (%)	Farmer/ Petty Trader (%)	Govt. Service/ Business (%)	Total (%)
Daily Labourer/ Traditional Parental	1 (04.0)	2 (04.2)	—	3 (02.0)
Farmer/ Private Employee	4 (16.0)	7 (14.5)	11 (14.3)	22 (14.7)
Government Service/ Business	20 (80.0)	39 (81.3)	66 (85.7)	125(83.3)
Total	**25 (100)**	**48 (100)**	**77 (100)**	**150 (100)**

Table 2.11 summarises the generational mobility with reference to occupational aspirations of the respondents. If daily labourer/private employee, farmer/petty trader and government service/business are ranked as low, medium and high occupations respectively, it can be seen from the table that the occupational aspirations of the youth on the whole indicate upward mobility. The vast majority (80 percent or more) of the respondents from all the three categories of parental occupation aspire for the high occupations of government service or business. It is, however, surprising to note that 11 (14.3 percent) out of the 77 respondents whose parental occupation was government service or business opted for the occupation of farmer/private employee.

Nevertheless, our data are insufficient to find out the actual realisation of the generational mobility in occupation. Aspirations of youth are usually higher than their expectations and occupational aspirations need not result in actual occupational attainment. So there may or may not be a positive correlation between structural factors such as family's socio-economic background and actual realisation of occupational aspirations of youth.

Spatial Mobility

Since migration or spatial mobility is one of the important means to realise the goals in life and one of the main characteristics of modernisation, it has been ascertained from the youth whether they would be aspiring to move out for work outside their locality, within India or abroad. Table 2.12 gives the information on the youth's aspirations for spatial mobility for work. Less than half (43.3 percent) of the youth in the sample prefer to work within their own locality, while the remaining 56.7 per cent of them think of moving out of their locality in pursuit of work. Those who aspire to go abroad for work constitute 40 per cent of the sample, whereas 16.7 per cent of the youth are aspiring to work outside their locality within India.

Table 2.12
Gender and Preferred Place of Occupation

	Gender		
Place Preferred:	Male (%)	Female (%)	Total (%)
Abroad	41(45.5)	19(31.6)	60(40)
Within locality	32(35.5)	33(55)	65(43.3)
Outside locality	17(18.8)	8(13.2)	25(16.6)
Total	**90(100)**	**60(100)**	**150(100)**

With respect to gender, the proportion of those who want to go abroad is higher among the male youth (45.5 percent) than among the female (31.7 percent), whereas majority (55 percent) of the female youth and about one third (35.6 percent) of the male youth want to work within their own locality. Compulsions of the roles of mother and house-wife within the family, and traditional restrictions on women's mobility could be the reasons why majority of the female respondents have shown their preference to work within their own locality. However, while ascertaining the motivation behind their eagerness to go abroad as many as 35 out of the 60 respondents who aspire for work abroad mentioned higher earning as the motivating factor.

Table 2.13
Gender and Stated Reasons for Going Abroad

	Gender		
Reasons:	Male (%)	Female (%)	Total (%)
To earn more money	26(63.4)	9(47.3)	35(58.3)
To achieve high status	7(17)	6(31.5)	13(21.6)
To keep pace with modern western life	8(19.5)	4(21)	12(20)
Total	**41(100)**	**19(100)**	**60(100)**

Out of the remaining 25 respondents seeking work abroad, 13 youth were inspired by the higher status in the foreign job and remaining 12 youth considered foreign job a means to keep pace with modern Western life. The data on the aspirations of spatial mobility indicate that the Ladakhi youth are gradually getting out of the constraints of the traditional social structure. All this makes us assume that what the young people today are looking for is the modern, Western and urban money oriented culture and life style which are increasingly appealing to them. They are seeking opportunities to break the traditional boundaries and pursue their aspirations that give them an identity of their own in the changing social situation.

Interests and Leisure Activities

Personal life style, that comprises the core of youth culture, is an area wherein the youth would like to exercise much of their options. In this area the youth want to enjoy considerable freedom from adult regulations. Most of them want to have fun and amusements among themselves outside of the regulated sphere of daily life, comprising of school and work situations. Their interest in activities of leisure and pleasure may be stronger as compared to adults, and it is this orientation that brings youth together. However, in discussing activities of leisure and pleasure as active features of the lives of youth, one must at the same time differentiate between more and less common activities. Certain activities are part of daily routines and are carried out regularly, probably even ritually. Other activities are less common and constitute a deviation from daily routines. One of the regular activities that, perhaps more than any other binds the day together is the use of mass media. For most of the literate people the day begins with reading the local newspaper in the morning; during the rest of the day the radio may be on; and in the evening people may watch television. Particularly among youth, mass media is very important and it is said that it survives mainly on the young urban market. That is why social scientists have attached significance to the use of films/music as an essential component of youth culture. Each sub-culture has tended to invent musical style that goes along with its general orientations. However, the contemporary films/musical currents owe their origin to indigenous as well as Western style. The youth today have the choice from this expanse of various traditions. The present study probed into the preferences of the youth in their activities of leisure and pleasure.

Nonetheless, while dealing with mass media we have confined ourselves to radio, television, news papers and magazines with a view to know how far our respondents have taken to these, and with what interests are they exposed to mass media.

Table 2.14
Degree of Exposure to Media (Radio and Television)

	Gender		
Degree of Exposure:	Male (%)	Female (%)	Total (%)
Daily	69(76.5)	48(79.6)	117(78)
Once or twice a day	14(15.5)	8(13.2)	22(14.6)
Don't listen/ watch or not interested	7(7.7)	4(6.6)	11(7.3)
Total	**90(100)**	**60(100)**	**150(100)**

On the basis of above data, we are attuned to that 78 percent of the respondents listen/ watch radio and television daily. Gender wise distribution of data reveals that frequency or degree of listening/ watching radio and T.V is more among female youth (79.6 percent) as compared to male. Another notable fact is that 7.3 percent of respondents indicated that they don't listen/ watch or are not interested in radio and television, which could partly or wholly be due to the inaccessibility to these means of entertainment and education or may be due to many other reasons. Or else radio and television as revealed in the field are not merely a channels of entertainment for young, but goes beyond in influencing their behaviour in day-to-day life. Much of the ideas about love, romance, courtship, songs and dialogue of the films influence and enter the patterns of young people's language and communication.

Table 2.15
Present Occupational Status and Preference of Films/ Music

Preferences:	Present Occupational Status		
	Student (%)	Non-student/ Working (%)	Total (%)
Indian films/ musical programmes	67(64.4)	21(60)	88 (63.3)
Folk films/ musical programmes	12(11.5)	10(28.6)	22(15.8)
Western or foreign films/ musical programmes	17(16.3)	3 (8.5)	20 (14.3)
Others (detective/ religious) programmes	8(7.6)	1(2.8)	9(6.4)
Total	**104 (100)**	**35 (100)**	**139 (100)**

Don't listen/ watch or not interested categories are not included.

Table 2.15 presents the distribution of the youth of the sample by their preference for leisure time activities. The data here show that majority (58.7 percent) of the youth prefer

Indian films/music, followed by another 14.7 per cent of the youth who like folk films/music. Only a minority (13.3 percent) of the youth have shown preference for western films/music. While many of the youth in Ladakh think of going abroad for seeking employment and making money as mentioned earlier, their preferences are for the Indian products in the case of amusements and leisure time activities.

Apart from radio and television or cinema, newspapers, magazines, novels and books etc., constitute print sources of mass media. These sources can't be a common media for all like radio and T.V, because to read newspaper or any print source of media requires a certain minimum level of literacy. In fact one of the best indicators of literacy is the ability to read newspaper. In view of such observations respondents were asked to indicate whether they can read and if so, it was assumed from the point of view of consequences of reading more important to know what type of material/ print media they are exposed to.

Table 2.16

Gender and Exposure to Print Media

Type of Material	Gender		
	Male (%)	Female (%)	Total (%)
Science magazines and papers	15(18)	8(14)	23(16.4)
Film magazines and paper	29(34.9)	21(36.8)	50(35.7)
Current affair magazines and papers	31(37.3)	25(43.8)	56(40)
Fiction magazines and papers	8(9.6)	3(5.2)	11(7.8)
Total	**83(100)**	**57(100)**	**w140(100)**

Not interested/ can't read categories are not included.

Here we find that the proportion of those who are attracted to read matters related to current affairs is higher (40 percent) followed by 35.7 percent of respondents, who prefer to read film magazines and papers. The gender wise distribution of data indicates that more female youth are interested in films and current affairs magazines and papers (36.8 and 43.8 percent respectively). This confirms the data given in table 2.14 whereby it is illustrated that more female youth are interested in radio and television. Thus it becomes suggestive that compared to male, female youth are more interested and consume mass media. Nevertheless, further analysis of the data in table 2.16 shows that compared to female, more male youth are attracted to science and fiction magazines and papers (18 and 9.6 percent respectively). By and large, it can be generalized that the main interest of youth centers around films and current affairs related materials.

There are also other leisure time activities among the youth. As revealed during the field study, gossip is the most common leisure time activity found among the youth of the study, because it is not bound by time and place.

Table 2.17
Gender and Leisure Time Activities

Activities:	Gender		
	Male (%)	Female (%)	Total (%)
Gossip	31(34.4)	29(48.1)	60(40)
Watch T.V	13(14.4)	12(19.9)	25(16.6)
Roaming around town	24(26.6)	5(8.3)	29(19.3)
Study together	7(7.7)	14(23.2)	21(14)
Play cards	15(16.6)	—	15(10)
Total	**90(100)**	**60(100)**	**150(100)**

Groups of youth could be seen conversing in the corridors near classrooms, even inside the library, at market places, in tea stalls, hotels, etc., and also roaming around the town which is but an extension of the exchange of conversation, chit-chat and gossip sessions. If gossip occupies such an important place in the time use pattern of the present youth, the inevitable question arises what goes into it. One is inclined to agree that peer group functions for young people as a "social womb", and is used to escape the demands from the world-at-large and for self-affirmation. In peer group one seeks mutual closeness as different from relationships with other independent individuals. However, with respect to gender, more female youth were seen indulging in gossip as the most favoured leisure time activity, whereas among male youth roaming around town and playing cards occupied more space. An inference which can be drawn from the above is that these leisure time activities of the youth are disorganised, in the sense that they spend most of the leisure time in activities like roaming around the town, playing cards and indulging in excessive gossip, which at certain points of time act as a source of conflict between them (youth) and their parents, a point that I shall be dealing with later in the chapter.

Dress Pattern and Food Habits

Dress pattern is an important means by which an individual discovers and expresses his/her identity. A significant function of clothing, especially for the adolescents and youth, is to assure their identity and sense of belongingness to peer groups. In contemporary days the "mediazation" process has contributed to changes in the consumption, dress and eating patterns of the present youth. For a number of young men and women jeans as a daily mode of dress have become a symbol of freedom, informality and expression of youthfulness. Similarly visits to hotels and restaurants, partying with friends, late night dinners, going to gym to shape body etc. are gaining increasing acceptance among the youth.

Table 2.18

Gender and Preference of Dress Pattern and Food Habits

	Gender		
Preference:	Male (%)	Female (%)	Total (%)
Local	25(27.7)	29(48.3)	54(36)
Western/foreign	65(72.2)	31(51.6)	96(64)
Total	**90(100)**	**60(100)**	**150(100)**

In the present study an enquiry was made into the dressing and eating patterns of the Ladakhi youth. Table 2.18 reveals that a large number (64 percent) of the youth in the sample prefer foreign/Western dress and eating patterns. Gender-wise data show that more male youth (72.2 percent) indicated their interest in foreign dress and eating patterns as compared to the females among whom 48.3 per cent preferred local dress and eating patterns.

While probing into the reasons for opting foreign dress and eating patterns, it was revealed that the main reasons given were that they found foreign/Western dress pattern more interesting, comfortable and superior than the local.

Table 2.19

Stated Reasons for Giving Preference to Western/ Foreign Dress Pattern and Food Habits

	Gender		
Reasons:	Male (%)	Female (%)	Total (%)
Makes one feel enlightened and belonging with peers	31(47.6)	11(35.4)	42(43.7)
More interesting, comfortable and superior than local	34(52.3)	20(64.5)	54(56.2)
Total	**65(100)**	**31(100)**	**96(100)**

Note: Those who give preference to local dress and eating pattern have not been included.

Besides, during interviews many respondents in general terms maintained that modern life style provides them fun without restrictions from elders. For some it is a mode of exhibition of their glamour, beauty, money and even influence primarily to impress the peers of the other sex, as a few of the respondents remarked: "We don't get much fun when the girls aren't around to watch."

Though there is a general orientation among youth towards going on diet or using other methods to improve their figure or physique, the food and drinking habits of youth are to a large extent influenced by their family and religious background. For example, a Muslim boy is free to experiment with non-vegetarian food, but in the matter of drinking liquor the odds are much more against him as compared to a Buddhist or Hindu boy. Therefore, the attitude towards non-vegetarianism and use of liquor varies from community to community. However, despite this, an interesting fact revealed during the field data collection was that food items like those of the Chinese, Korean or Japanese are popular among the youth in Ladakh.

Conflict with Parents

Intergenerational conflict is a common phenomenon in a changing social situation. As the youth increasingly get exposed to new values and styles of living, they are likely to come into conflict with their parents. A small attempt was made in the present study to look into this aspect of the youth in Ladakh. Table 2.20 presents its findings. As expected, all the youth in the sample have experienced conflict with parents on some issue or other.

Table 2.20

Gender and Causes of Clash and Conflict with Parents

	Gender		
Causes:	Male (%)	Female (%)	Total (%)
Money matters	31(34.4)	23(38.1)	54(36)
Religious beliefs	15(16.6)	5(8.3)	20(13.3)
Political beliefs	4(4.4)	3(4.9)	7(4.6)
Friendship matters	29(32.1)	20(33.2)	49(32.6)
Others (work matters etc.)	11(12.2)	9(14.9)	20(13.3)
Total	**90(100)**	**60(100)**	**150(100)**

Matters related to money and friendships appeared to be the main issues involved in conflict with parents, and were in the case of 36 and 32.7 per cent of the sample respectively. The issue of religious beliefs accounted for conflict in the case of 13.3 per cent of the youth. Change in the style of life, and attitudinal and behavioural changes among the youth towards sex and religion are likely to generate intergenerational conflict and clash, because the youth today are increasingly in favour of boys and girls meeting before marriage and maintaining close contact which may not be to the liking of the elders in the society. Besides, spending much time with friends, bringing friends home too often and not frequently visiting a place of worship etc. could be reasons of conflict with parents. The combination of these factors, as revealed in the discussion with a number of respondents, act as the chief negative factor in befriending members of the opposite sex and peer formation. There is hardly any gender difference in the matter of the issues involved in conflict with parents, except in the issue of religious beliefs. While 16.7 per cent of the male youth reported religious beliefs as an issue in conflict with parents, only 8.3 per cent of the female youth had the similar experience.

On the whole, it appears that the life style of the youth which involves spending on things considered as luxurious or conspicuous consumption by the parents is the main source of conflict of youth with parents.

Table 2.21
Gender and Stated Reasons of Money Matter Clashes

	Gender		
Reasons:	Male (%)	Female (%)	Total (%)
Don't give enough money	21(67.7)	12(52.1)	33(61.1)
Don't allow to consume costly items	9(29.0)	11(47.8)	20(37.0)
Can't say	1(3.2)	—	1(1.8)
Total	**31(100)**	**23(100)**	**54(100)**

As many as 53 out of the 54 respondents who mentioned money as the issue in conflict said that they did not get enough pocket money from parents or the parents did not allow them to consume costly items. Since youth is a period of strong change when one is wide open to all sorts of new and modern influences, especially due to the development in fashion industry, youth may adopt a new consumption pattern and think it necessary to change frequently one's wardrobe including jewellery and perfume, and even leisure time activities when fashion changes. On the one hand the life cycle of the fashion products is much shorter and on the other, fashion is linked to social strata and determined largely by economic capital. The consumption pattern of the youth may not be approved by their parents. Further it could be a burden on low income families which the parents may find it difficult to bear.

Beliefs and Value Orientations

In the age of free and frequent contact and communication between people of various countries and cultures, the impact on thinking, beliefs and behaviour pattern is readily seen. In this process much is said about youth, who are regarded to be not in a mood to conform to styles of life of older generations rather they lay much stress on individual freedom, individual initiative, and individual life etc. In light of this, an understanding of the perspective of the youth on certain important issues has been dealt in the present study.

Premarital Sex

Over the years the standards of relationship between sexes have been gradually becoming liberal. This is particularly true of the youth and today one finds teenagers not shy of dating or going out and interacting with the opposite sex as if they are no longer restricted by the conventional view to preserve the big 'V' of virginity for the nuptial night. Dating is getting increasingly viewed as a fashion symbol in many of the urban communities. In view of these modern trends, the youth of the present study were asked what they thought about premarital sex. Table 2.22 presents the results of this enquiry.

Table 2.22
Gender and Views about Pre-marital Sex

Views:	Gender		
	Male (%)	Female (%)	Total (%)
It is against religion	42(46.6)	47(78.3)	89(59.3)
It is not so much a moral issue	3(3.3)	1(1.6)	4(2.6)
Experimenting with sex	31(34.4)	3(5)	34(22.6)
All about being comfortable with the person one loves	14(15.5)	9(15)	23(15.3)
Total	**90(100)**	**60(100)**	**150(100)**

Data in table 2.22 indicate that majority (59.3 percent) of the youth in the sample maintain that premarital sex is against religion. Contrary to this, the remaining 40.7 per cent of the respondents did not disapprove it on religious or moral ground. While 34 (22.7 percent) of the youth in the sample considered it as experimenting with sex, 23 (15.3 percent) of the youth viewed premarital sex as a matter of personal choice and being comfortable with the person one shares an intimate relationship with. The following view expressed during the interview is in accordance with this position. "You can marry only when a right person comes along. But suppose that doesn't happen, you can't deprive yourself of other pleasures. If you love someone and are sexually attracted to him/her, why deny yourself the pleasure?" There is some difference between the male and female youth on the religious outlook towards premarital sex. While 78.3 per cent female youth think sexual encounter before marriage to be against religion, 46.6 per cent of the male youth are in agreement with the same.

Since, adolescence and youth is characterized by "an open psychic structure", being curious to test out all sorts of things even the forbidden, mass media plays a significant part in bringing sweeping changes in behaviour and attitude of young people and contributes directly or indirectly to "boundary crises", between what is permitted and what is not permitted, because mass media largely stand for emotional empathy, pleasure and devotion-values sharply contrasting with those of the adult world, working life, school and to a degree also with the family's demand for discipline, punctuality and rationality.

Table 2.23
Media Exposure and Views about Pre-marital Sex

	Media Exposure			
Views:	High (%)	Medium (%)	Low (%)	Total (%)
It is against religion	66(56.4)	16(72.7)	7(63.6)	89(59.3)
It is not so much a moral issue	2(1.7)	1(4.5)	1(9)	4(2.6)
Experimenting with sex	31(26.4)	1(4.5)	2(18)	34(22.6)
All about being comfortable with the person one loves	18 (15.3)	4 (18.1)	1 (9)	23 (15.3)
Total	117 (100)	22 (100)	11 (100)	150 (100)

Table 2.23 gives the comparison between the distribution of youth according to their media exposure and their views about premarital sex. To begin with, we find respondents in high category of media exposure shown greater openness in such relations and do not consider anything wrong in

having sex before marriage, whereas those having medium level of exposure are to large extent reserved in these regards. However, further analysis of data indicates certain amount of variations in the views of respondents accordingly which may be either due to their subjective meanings and understanding or may be argued are the manifestations of positive as well as negative implications of mass media, because our data shows that 63.6 percent respondents from not interested/ low media exposure category viewed premarital sex against religion, whereas 56.4 percent from high media exposure category viewed the same. This may be assumed as the manifestation of negative impacts of mass media. Simultaneously further analysis reveals that one percent from low media exposure category and only 1.7 percent from high media exposure category followed by 4.5 percent respondents from medium level exposure category consider premarital sex not so much a moral issue.

Altogether, it shows as the media exposure increases, knowledge about certain life fields (morality) increases but at the same time this increase in media exposure has negative impact on sexual life of an individual. So one can safely presume that on the one hand mass media is a great source of information, entertainment and connectivity, on the other it has brought changes in the moral fabric of the society. Day by day adolescents and youth are getting increasingly exposed to pornographic material and cyber friendships with shady characters etc. Particularly today multimedia messaging system of cell phones has entirely radicalized the ideas and attitude of youth towards sexual orientation.

Age at Marriage

Marriage is perceived by sociologists as a system of roles of a man and a woman whose union has been given social sanction as husband and wife. However, the readiness for marriage involves ability to take on the responsibilities of marriage. One important factor which determines readiness for marriage for a person is his maturity. A matured person is one who has developed the ability to establish and maintain personal relationship. Nevertheless the question still remains that at what age a person should marry? The question is partly answered by legislators and partly by the opinions of the people about the age one should marry?

Table 2.24

Gender and Opinion for Age at Marriage

	Gender		
Age (Years):	Male (%)	Female (%)	Total (%)
18-21	17(18.8)	8(13.3)	25(16.6)
22-25	47(52.2)	41(68.3)	88(58.6)
25 & above	26(28.8)	11(18.3)	37(24.6)
Total	**90(100)**	**60(100)**	**150(100)**

On the basis of the analysis of the percentage distribution, the data in table 2.24 reveals that the majority of youth both male and female are of the opinion that the age of marriage should be between 22-25 years. Greater consensus is found among female youth in this respect. Nonetheless it shows that young people of today, who have been out in the world and who hear and know much about marriage can't keep their minds blank on this matter. Many times during interviews when it came to the qualities of life-partner it was found that youth don't differ much with regard to number of qualities they look for their future partner as their choice is predominantly confined to four characteristics of their personality namely character, beauty, intelligence, and education. Thus, they have learnt the importance of new social values and making their—selves to be less orthodox in their ways. This further indicates that their future orientations concern the belief that it is worthwhile to plan things and to sacrifice present gratification for the future well being.

In some cases however, it is love and romance which provide shelter to these young people who are otherwise busy and struggling to become self sufficient and interested in marriage at late twenties. Under this system of love and romance both lover and beloved feel that they got sufficient maturity to decide about their future life. They therefore argue that let their choice and word be final in such matters and not those of their parents, because love is considered as the essence of happiness in marriage. In contemporary days however, there are certain issues related to love and romance like inter-religious marriages and premarital sex etc. Since inter-religious marriages involve a sociological problem of assimilation and adjustment, its discussion has become a lively issue in the discipline of sociology.

Table 2.25

Gender and Opinion for Inter-Religious Love Marriage

Opinion:	Male (%)	Female (%)	Total (%)
Religion more important in choosing life-partner	43(47.7)	56(93)	99(66)
Religion not important in choosing life-partner	17(18.8)	2(3.3)	19(12.6)
Want to encourage inter-religious marriages	21(23.2)	—	21(14)
Can't go against parents and relatives wish	2(2.2)	2(3.3)	4(2.6)
Don't bother about parents and relatives wish	7(7.7)	—	7(4.6)
Total	**90(100)**	**60(100)**	**150(100)**

Looking at the data it is found that 12.6 percent youth don't consider religion important in marriage and 14 percent youth want to encourage inter-religious marriages. Hence, all these youth have no objection in marrying outside their religion. Gender wise data reveals that more male as compared to female youth favour inter religious marriages. Whereas formerly in Ladakh, there was some flexibility in choosing the life-partner outside ones religious group, today many young people are also prepared to break through the bonds of religion if mutual love, romance or attraction demands it, as our data indicates that 4.6 percent youth don't bother about parents and relatives wish and stress the individuals supreme right to love and be loved in a romantic sense. However, the fact is that such inter-ethnic marital alliances particularly between Buddhists and Muslims, which were not taken up with any seriousness at one time, got a severe jolt after the Sabu village incident in 1960's in Leh, when an inter-ethnic marriage was given a political colour leading to societal conflict and even violence in 1969. In subsequent years it has led to the stoppage of such marital alliances, because of the risk involved, and since the partners entering such a union had done so for individual reasons alone without familial and social backup, it tends to be more fragile and unstable.

Gender

Societies are continually changing its course and adopting itself to new conditions, in this process, role and status of women is continuously changing. The borderlines between which is permitted and suitable for each gender changed. Today most women have entered in different professions and have their own income and social environment outside the family. In light of these observations, subjects of our study were asked to express their opinion concerning the same.

Table 2.26
Opinion for Equal Gender Status

	Gender		
Opinion:	Male (%)	Female (%)	Total (%)
Pertaining to Yes			
Enable women to tackle socio-economic problems	58 (64.4)	34 (56.6)	92 (61.3)
Reduce crime rate against women	21 (23.3)	24 (40)	45 (30)
Total			**137(91.3)**
Pertaining to No			
Destroy religious and moral fabric of society	3(3.3)	1(1.6)	4(2.6)
Increases crime rate against women	2(2.2)	1(1.6)	3(2)
Increases unemployment among men	6(6.6)	—	6(4)
Total			**13(8.6)**
Total	**90(100)**	**60(100)**	**150(100)**

We find overwhelming majority of 91.3 percent respondents, who have shown favourable attitude towards equal gender status. While among them 61.3 percent argued that equal gender status would enable women to tackle socio-economic problems, 30 percent hold that it will reduce crime rate against women. Further analysis of data however shows that there are also 8.6 percent respondents who are not in favour of equal gender status. The reasons they have maintained for the same are not less rational and less thought provoking, but not more secular and democratic as compared to the arguments of first category. Moreover among the second category pertaining to 'no,' gender wise distribution indicates that more male youth disapproved such equal status.

However considered as a whole, it can be concluded that there is a large change in idea and attitude among present day Ladakhi youth regarding equal gender status, who argue and favour the cultural freedom to women along the lines best suited to them.

3

Ladakhi Youth: Emerging Trends and Policy Implications

Youth is what is young and what belongs to the future, and young people have repeatedly been associated with what is new in culture. On the negative side, youth is often associated with the dangers of the future. Specifically when fear of the unknown is coupled with a culturally pessimistic diagnosis of degeneration, the morals and norms of youth become sure signs of the sins and transgressions of modernity. Such reactions are especially strong when youth and the media interact. However, on the positive side, youth has long been associated with future hopes, promises of a new life and the progress of modernity. Young people really are the adults of future; some of them will wield power and be decision-makers. Their biological, psychodynamic, socially and culturally-conditioned flexibility also give them (youth) a strong, seismographic ability to register deep, but hidden social movements and to express these in the clear language of style.

Putting all the pieces together, youth in the current times come across as both individualistic fun-seekers and frail pragmatists and we would argue that these are two sides of the same coin. A coin, however, can't separate its two sides, yet youth do to a great degree. In the private spheres, especially when they are dealing with their parents and loved ones, they are individualistic, self-centered, bold in their pursuit of fun, and fashionable. In the spheres of public life, on the other hand, they are bluntly pragmatic, choosing the safest way to maximize their educational returns, income, power and prestige etc. To reach these goals, they are competitive and conscious of rights, however the socio-economic conditions under with they live are found to be influencing their life chances.

The results of our study clearly indicate that the incidence of low educational level of youth is mainly related to their socio-economic background. On the one hand majority of respondents either undergraduate or pursuing degrees in different academic, technical and professional courses were belonging to parents with high educational level and on the other, youth either illiterate or having primary or middle level of education were belonging to parents with low level of education or having no education. Similarly parent's monthly income and present occupational status of our respondents shows a relationship, wherein more incidences of non-student/ working youth were from low income category, whereas student youth largely belonged to high and medium income categories respectively, which again confirms that difference in educational and occupational status of youth can be attributed to the variation in their socio-economic background.

Although this empirical analysis points out how things go together and how social space is constructed on the basis of socio-economic capital. The image of one's aim of life, as to what one is and what one wants to attain or become in life, there doesn't seem to be any association between the real and ideal. Because in recent years economic changes have set in motion certain processes, having substantial impact on the orientations and aspirations of youth in particular. Putting more effort and faith in education than ever before, youth are continually changing their orientations of life and adopting itself to new conditions. Education as one of the few sure roads to economic progress has become a contemporary creed. The perspective of majority of our respondents about the principal goal of education reflects the modern Western and market driven notion about education. Contrary to the academic and religious oriented studies, in view of their economic development, occupational and social mobility, they consider these courses more useful and don't espouse to greater extent the traditional view of education for the development of man's inner self.

However, minimizing this role of education and with the inculcation of rational means-ends calculations, and new attitude to wealth and work etc., has inevitably affected traditional occupational roles and aspirations of youth in particular. In the areas of job preferences our study revealed that 45.3 percent youth would like to opt for business followed by 38 percent who would like to go for government jobs. With respect to gender preference to business is more among male youth, whereas among female ones, it is government job, which finds more place. Equally on the basis of present occupational status (student or non-student/working) of the respondents, larger proportion of Ladakhi youth show more favourable and popular attitude and interest in business. Their stated reasons for giving preference to business clearly indicates that among vast majority of them work and occupation have assumed utmost economic significance, which is reflected in their fast changing values and attitudes.

Moreover, it is revealed in our study that occupational aspirations of Ladakhi youth are upward however; there is not any marked relationship between the father's occupation and occupational aspirations of these youth as our respondents from all occupational backgrounds: low, medium and high, inclined almost equally to go for government job and business. Similarly, in the case of farming and private sector jobs the trend is same. Therefore, it partially sustains and demonstrates the validity of the related hypotheses that individual choices and desires are becoming more important than the structural factors, and suggests that young people no longer follow their parent's footsteps, but instead are looking to choose more independent life-styles.

While occupational aspirations of Ladakhi youth are high, however this can't be the good predictor of actual occupational attainment. Thus, the chances of goal attainment don't appear to be quite encouraging and this can be one of the reasons why 40 percent youth as our study showed, want to move out and go abroad. Nonetheless, while ascertaining the motivations behind their willingness to go abroad, the most obvious element is the acquisition of material rewards and urban life-style, wherein traditional socio-economic factors increasingly lose their significance in the choice of life-style: the choice becomes ever more personal.

Personal life-style is therefore, an area in which Ladakhi youth enjoy considerable freedom from adult regulations. But still they choose their activities in accord with what other young people with corresponding positions in the social space do. What is notable among present day Ladakhi youth is an entertainment orientation, interest in leisure and pleasure, and it is this orientation (with influences coming from the mass media) which unites youth. With regards to mass media, our study revealed that vast majority of youth at relatively considerable degree is exposed to radio, T.V, newspapers and magazines etc. However compared to male, more female youth consume the mass media. It may be added here that on the whole main interest of youth centers round film/ music and current affairs related programmes and materials.

In the social areas of dress pattern and food habits our study showed that large percentage of Ladakhi youth do have a less inclination towards traditional dress and eating patterns and it is more true about male youth. Probing into the reasons for opting the same, yielded that more female youth consider foreign dress and eating patterns more comfortable and superior than their local, hence developing a subtle contempt for their own culture in the process. This confirms the validity of the hypotheses that Western culture is taking precedence over local culture and influences the young people to large extent in their day to day life.

So far as the leisure time activities of these youth are concerned, leisure time gossip is the most favoured activity. Gender wise data, however shows that more female youth consider indulging in gossip most interesting, whereas among male youth roaming and playing cards occupy most space. It is important to note here that these activities in certain cases are unsystematic and may involve an experience of odds with the parents and elders. Our study manifests that money matters are the main source followed by friendship matters and religious beliefs in which much conflict between parents and their wards usually arise. However, at the same time, it is also revealed that today's Ladakhi youth have learnt the importance of new social values and making their-selves to be less orthodox in their ways. Majority of youth viewed 22-25 years age more suitable for entering into the marriage, however, more consensus is found among female youth in this regard, which indicate their concern in belief that it is worthwhile to plan things. Furthermore, it is also found in the study that 12.6 percent of Ladakhi youth don't consider religion important while choosing a life partner and 14 percent youth want to encourage inter-religious marriages. But the fact is that such alliances particularly between Buddhists and Muslims involve risk and are discouraged for certain reasons like inter-ethnic violence and conflicts etc.

Since adolescence and youth is characterized by being curious to test all new and even forbidden, the study showed that collectively 40.5 percent youth consider nothing wrong with pre-marital sex. However, gender wise analysis indicates that female youth are to a greater extent reserved in such relationships. While comparing the degree of media exposure and the views of youth about premarital sex, present study showed as the media exposure increases it does influence their sexual life particularly their attitude towards pre-marital sex.

Lastly, but not of the least importance, the study underlines the healthy frame of mind and outlook of the Ladakhi youth, preferring equal gender status and projecting values significantly different from their elders. As such this study reveals some visionary and intellectual maturity on the part of youth, there is however still much to be accomplished in this direction, because today as never before in the history of man, the individual is more than a national citizen, whose thinking, action and deeds are not only shaped by local and national forces: but they bear the imprint of global influences. The advent of global values into the life of national and local society is an undeniable reality to which present study too demonstrates.

It is youth who stands at the centre of this panorama of change, they are in the cradle of globalization, liberalization and privatization, and should be prepared to face its challenges, because today's youth is tomorrow's world leader and peace setter, and every society depends a great deal on its young men and women. It is helpful to have youth coming forward with the sole intension of doing the right thing. However, much depends upon the capacity of the dominant establishments of the society to satisfy the aspirations of the young and in the process of doing so, evolve an adequate youth policy and programme in this respect. Although we are not policy planners or futurists, remaining within the broader frame work of Ladakhi culture and present changing scenario, on the basis of empirical and observational demonstrations of the present study, we have offered some suggestions to channelise youth's energies, idealism and their healthy aspirations towards developmentalism.

Policy Implications

As far as Ladahki youth are concerned there could be several possibilities to channelise youth's energies and aspirations. First, youth must have easy access to a modern system of education that offers a variety of choices to suit individual needs and encourages self study, free expression and creativity. Career counselling at different stages of their education should be part of this system of education so as to realise the dissociation of degree or diploma from job. For the non-student youth or youth who have not acquired a minimum educational level, short-term training programmes in vocational or technical skills may be provided in order to impart skills and develop their productive potential to become dynamic members of their community.

Young people should be encouraged to explore a life style that is based on certain values, such as restraint, austerity and regulated consumption, so that they do not become victims to the onslaught of globalisation and consumerism. They also need to be rooted in certain attitudes and orientation to the basic social institutions such as the family, so that they do not become socially alienated but learn to live within the family and community in a pleasant and harmonious atmosphere.

The potentialities of the youth should be fruitfully channelled and utilised within the community. They may be associated actively in the process of evolving and managing cultural activities and programmes, and thus enabled to realise and appreciate the cultural heritage of their society and its unique Ladakhi identity. Today the task before the society is to enable its youth to perform their significant role within the changing social scenario.

Youth need guidance, advice and help with regard to intergenerational conflict and community life. Therefore, socio-psychological and health counselling should be introduced as one of the activities in educational institutions and youth serving organizations like Nehru Yuvak Kendra (NYKS), Student Educational And Cultural Movement Of Ladakh (SECMOL) and Women Alliance Of Ladakh (WAL) etc.

Young people should be increasingly entrusted with positions of responsibility and authority. At present the peak of creativity is reached at fairly early age, but traditional habits and respect for age and experience often works against the recognition of the capacity and merit of youth. A marked change of outlook and practice is now called for.

The content on the electronic media is not necessarily negative alone, unfortunately is very misleading for adolescents and youth. Therefore, there is need for helping parents on how to help children to deal with media. Merely telling children not to watch television is no solution. Rather helping children to take responsibility when it comes to watching T.V and other media identifies two major areas of concern to parents: content-what children watch and time-how much time is spent in front of audio-visual media. Parents must also focus greater attention in providing socialization into the productive use of leisure time so that unintended consequences like wandering, roaming and playing cards etc. can be avoided at early.

Ladakh Autonomous Hill Development Council (LAHDC) Leh, Ministry of Youth Affairs and Sports and Ministry of Culture (Govt. of India) should look forward to provide more funding assistance to local youth serving NGOs and organizations so that additional sports activities are conducted, and interest and talent of youth in the field of games and sports can be encouraged and strengthened.

All youth serving agencies, organizations and NGOs presently operating in rural as well as urban areas of the

Ladakh such as NYKs (Nehru Yuvak Kendra), SECMOL (Student Educational And Cultural Movement Of Ladakh), WAL (Women Alliance of Ladakh), SBWS (SKARCHEN Balti Welfare Society), LEDG (Ladakh Ecological Development Group) and Al-Zohra a Shia Muslim Women's Alliance, need to promote and encourage an element of respect for Ladakhi culture, to counter the disenchantment that many young people felt about their own local culture.

Lastly but not of the least importance, to triumph, youth need a vision and plan. Vision means the capacity of an individual to define the focus for future growth and development in all spheres. History has proved that nobody can become great without a vision and mission. All the great men of the world have their own vision which acts a key to open the heart of the modern youth. Recently, *VANI* (Voluntary Action Network India) has brought out a book titled, *India's Living Legends*, Savants of Voluntary Action (2002). In its foreword, his holiness the Dalai Lama has strongly recommended that said book will act as a catalyst in promoting social service and building a vision, especially among the youth.

> *As long as living beings remain,*
> *As long as space endures,*
> *May I too remain?*
> *To dispel the miseries of the world,*

Modern youth should be made aware of the teachings of great people like the Buddha, Prophet Mohammad, Jesus and living legends like Dalai Lama etc., which can give them the spiritual view of the life, and at the same time provide them enough role models in order to understand this life better in a holistic manner, so that there can be peace and prosperity in the world of youth and the world community at large. We would like to end with a beautiful quotation from Mao Tsetung's speech:

> The world is yours, as well as ours, but in the last analysis, it is yours, you young people, full of vigour and vitality, are in the bloom of life, like the sun at eight or nine in the morning (Yedla, 1992:29)

4

Understanding Youth Transitions in Kashmir: A Theoretical Discourse

Contemporary discursive interpretations of youth transitions have been widely influenced by sociological preoccupations with individualisation and its social and political implications (Beck and Beck-Gernsheim, 2002; Brannen and Nilsen, 2002; 2005; Roberts, 2012; Threadgold and Nilan, 2009; Woodman, 2010). Arguably, this theorising reflects a shift to reflexive or late modernity and has been very influential in contemporary sociological analysis (Bhat, 2013). It entails a regression in the coherence and certainty of once-established patterns of social (re)production, and a corresponding increase in individuals' capacity for self-determination (Beck, 1992; Giddens, 1991). More specifically, it has been argued that new ways of life now require people to 'produce, stage and cobble together their biographies' themselves (Beck, 1994: 13).

Within this discourse, the structural context for individual decision-making is portrayed as de-traditionalised. The individual's biographical development is left with no standard to follow and is particularly shown to be constructed without recourse to the lives of previous generations. Giddens (1994) demonstrates how in a de-traditionalised society, choices and decisions by rational arguments are key notions for understanding such processes at the individual level. As individual choices and decisions have become central, "choice biography" is said to replace "standard biography". The latter refers to the shaping of the life-course in traditional society, where people's origins largely determined their destiny and influenced which lines to follow. In late modernity, it is claimed that aspects of origin and particularly social class no longer have the same structuring role they once had. Major proponents of the "individualisation thesis" have branded social class as a "zombie variable" (Beck, 2002) or "shell institution" (Giddens, 1999). Beck (1992: 127-37) claims that individualised processes of making choices and decisions continue over the whole life-course of individuals.

Nowhere is this emphasis on individualised life chances more fully expressed than in sociologies of youth. Recent work in this field frequently emphasises three interlinked but distinct themes regarding young people's lives: the decline of class, reflexive identities and transformation in young people's political strategies (see Jeffrey, 2008). Young people are described as approaching and experiencing their lives in the present. Planning for their future, essentially as responsible individuals with the freedom to make their own decisions, they are in essence portrayed as acting 'to construct their own biographies on their own accounts' (Chisholm and du Bois-Reymond, 1993: 260). Youth transitions are also perceived as more open-ended and fluid, reflecting a freeing up of established patterns of transitions, wherein youth are expected to individually tailor and navigate their pathways to adulthood.

One major theoretical repercussion of this discourse is that young people are understood as living outside traditional social structures, in a context with intensified individualist values. Roberts (2010) argues that for the individualisation thesis structural constraints are either absent or very much secondary to agency. This means structural context is downplayed, while obeisance is paid to the new orthodoxy of agency. As Brannen and Nilsen (2005: 422) point out, this is problematic:

Individualisation theory emphasises the agency side of the classic sociological dynamic—between the individual and society—and downplays structure. When discussing how people construct their own life course trajectories, how they make choices and decisions and cobble together do-it-yourself biographies, little reference is made to the availability of resources to do so.

While it remains true that social change influences the lives of people in general and young people in particular, giving way to 'management through negotiation' and 'choice by rational arguments' seem to privilege individualisation. However, it strongly appears that reflexive/late-modernists have overstated these changes and the significance of individual reflexivity in young people's lives. To ignore structure may overlook the possibility of inequalities and differences in resources that are systemic and structural, rather than individual. Secondly, the individualisation thesis seems to take for granted an affluent society, ignoring structures that create inequality in many young people's ability to choose. Hence, it makes no distinction between consumption for basic needs and consumption for cultural choice (Jones and Wallace, 1992: 121-3).

Furthermore, as late-modernity advocates argue that time and space are lifted out of local context, or are disembedded, the place where you live is seen as less important than earlier. Late-modernists, therefore, tend to present their conclusions as universally applicable to contemporary youth, ignoring the fact that young people even in the global world are bounded by diverse social and cultural contexts. They live and learn somewhere with somebody. Setbacks and crisis in their life trajectories have come to be understood as individual inadequacies, rather than outcomes of social and economic restraints and processes that sustain inequality. There is, however, little doubt that unemployment, for example, remains often the experience of socio-economically marginalised individuals. In this context, Furlong and Cartmel (1997: 2-8) hold that existing patterns of inequality are simply being reproduced in different ways. Traditional determinants still have a powerful effect on the life trajectories of young people and cannot simply be ignored or their casual consequences denied.

The claims of the individualisation thesis around the contemporary irrelevance of class also ring void, given the increasingly escalating gap between rich and poor in contexts where social inequalities still seem to follow predictable patterns (Evans, 2007; Teese, 2000), and social mobility rates are almost static (Paxton and Dixon, 2004). Given such findings, there has been renewed interest in class analysis, in relation to the constitution of economic classes, the casual effects of class situations, the formation of social class and patterns of class awareness (Scott, 2002). Much of this revisionist work has been influenced by the work of Pierre Bourdieu (1930-2002), whose approach may be seen as blending, through his conceptual trilogy of field, capital and habitus, both economic and symbolic (cultural) forms of social differentiation and inequality. Expressly, in some recent sociologies of youth (Adams, 2006; Lehmann, 2007), Bourdieu's original theorising, particularly his practice theories and the concept of habitus, are applied as important analytical tools to understand continuing inequalities. Hence the two key tropes which have surfaced in the sociology of youth in recent years are typically clustered around the concepts of self-reflexivity and habitus.

At the theoretical level, this chapter highlights the continuing value and relevance of Bourdieu's work for an understanding of the experiences and trajectories of youth transitions in North India. A brief discussion of Bourdieu's stance on social reproduction below is followed by a section on methodology. The key arguments are then developed through major evidence from our data samples involving Kashmiri youth. It is argued that 'class analysis' still carries immense significance and remains a central analytical element in the analysis of youth transitions. Chapter concludes with some broad generalisations relating to contemporary youth research.

Habitus and Social Reproduction

Most of Bourdieu's work is embedded in elaborate attempts to account for the reproduction of power and privilege that accompanies the inequitable distribution and utility of social, economic and cultural capitals across social classes. He demonstrated that social space is constructed on the basis of the concept of three forms of capital, economic, social and cultural. These are distributed variably across populations according to class, which determines 'the chances of success for practice' (Bourdieu, 1986: 242).

In late modernity, this distribution can arguably be reduced to a relationship between educational attainment and cultural practice, as the capacity to engage in cultural practice is received in educational experience. Given cultural practices are coded, and therefore only accessible to those who have the key to the code, education becomes a key element for individual empowerment. As this educational key is differentially distributed according to social order, Bourdieu (1984: 14-18) argued that only persons in cultured families with certain refined tastes have access to this key, since cultural capital facilitates success in the fields of education, lifestyle and 'taste'. It includes resources such as verbal facility, general cultural awareness, aesthetic preferences, information and educational credentials (Swartz, 1997: 75). Moreover, it is 'differently formed in accordance with the different experiences and conditions of existence of the different social classes' (Bennett, Emmison and Frow, 1999: 11).

Bourdieu (1984: 171) further held that one's position in social space conditions the 'habitus' or living space. Habitus, a crucial concept at the heart of Bourdieu's sociology, is the system of interconnected dispositions that help us interpret our surrounding world. While each individual's habitus is unique, similar experiences tend to make it possible to refer to 'class habitus' (Bourdieu, 1984), an array of inherited dispositions that condition bodily movement, taste and judgments, according to class position. The primary basis for this conditioning is babyhood experience, in which the practices of parents regulate their interaction with the young child.

Habitus is thus constructed as an act of 'negotiation' that parents conduct in their everyday social life, keeping in view their material conditions of existence. When these conditions are unchanged, similar acts of negotiation result in a set of established dispositions for children to act in certain ways, specifying such action patterns as social distance, aspirations, body language, appropriate relationships, and so on. Hence, the habitus of the child reproduces the habitus of the parents.

Consequently the habitus develops into a way-of-doing things common to all those in a particular position. It generates schemes by which cultural objects are classified and differentiated (e.g. high/low, rich/poor), and standards of appreciation and evaluation, which allow an individual to express preferences, and which convey a 'sense of one's place', a feeling for one's own possibilities and limitations (Waters, 1994: 198-202). Objective constraints are in this way reinforced by perceptions.

These key concepts of Bourdieu are highly relevant for explaining why most working class youths still expect to get working class jobs, while the youth of the professional-managerial class expect to pursue professional-managerial and technical careers. Indeed we identified such normalisation in our data, presented further below.

Young People and Social Change in Kashmir

Certainly at the beginning of the new millennium, important social changes in local structures have taken place globally. Arguably the central driving force behind these rapid changes that are reshaping modern societies and the world order is globalisation, with most significant impacts on young people. Wulff (1995: 10) argues:

[. . .] When it comes to globalisation or transnational connections youth cultures are in the forefront of theoretical interest. Youth, their ideas and commodities move easily across national boundaries, shaping and being shaped by all kinds of structures and meanings.

Young Kashmiris do not live in isolation. Being on the cusp of change, they also represent a multiplicity of aspirations, worldviews and interests (Rather and Bhat, 2011). Like many beautiful, largely self-sufficient regions in the world, Kashmir has been influenced by external forces that caused massive and rapid social transformations. At the core of this phenomenon are ongoing processes of modernisation and the linkage of a traditional subsistence economy with regional and national markets, tourism and state interventions. In this milieu of change, there has been a tremendous rise in the level of aspirations of the general masses in Kashmir. Consumerism, commodification of lifestyle and product-hungry mentality have surfaced, while much declining interest in agricultural pursuits or blue-collar jobs is revealed. Contrarily a high priority is given to government jobs, linked to notions of what constitutes education (e.g. see 2nd chapter). As elsewhere, an educated person becomes an increasingly important focus for processes of identity formation. Certainly in this respect, the uncertainty in determining which qualifications and key competencies are necessary for a 'satisfactory life in a well-functioning society' (Rychen and Salganik, 2003) has nullified many conventional future aspirations in Kashmir.

Given this backdrop, combined with the rise of meritocracy, parenting has shown a considerable change over the last decade in Kashmir. Parents across a wide range of social backgrounds put into practice a variety of strategies to give their children exposure to a broader and wider curriculum, which by repercussion has resulted in increased privatisation of education. Professional and technical education is surfacing as a major modern social prerequisite in the life-course trajectories of young people, whether with an eye to compete in the labour market, the matrimonial market, or attaining high social recognition.

Consistent with reports of the Census (2011), educational participation in Jammu and Kashmir increased by 13 per cent in the last decade, implying increases in post-compulsory education and mounting pressure on government jobs. As Dore (1976) predicted long ago in his analysis of 'diploma disease', the combination of rising education and declining opportunities for secure salaried employment has increased feelings of frustration, inadequacy and failure among young people in many parts of the 'third world' (Bhat and Rather, 2012).

Hence, with the growth in post-compulsory educational participation but scanty employment opportunities, the pressure on young people to make rational choices is greater today than a few decades ago. This leads to what Giddens (1994: 75) accurately formulated when he wrote that people 'have no choice but to choose how to be and how to act'. However, this tells us little about the extent of autonomy.

The other major aspect of individualised agency in the lives of young people in Kashmir occurs in the domain of the cultural sphere. Owing to media-generated preferences, growing consumerism and the penchant for something new, cultural meandering among Kashmiri youth has meant that fashions, simulations and leisure culture are emerging as a lynchpin of social cohesion, cultural survival and markers of modernity. We could call it a 'new rigidity', because on the one hand traditional hierarchies of cultural preferences are now seen as only partially valid, while people hunt and exhibit their 'cultural' and 'social' individualised choices, to appear in the eyes of others as they want to be. To maintain one's standing, these lifestyle choices have become more important as a 'new rigidity' in terms of dress patterns, sports, media consumption and food habits. This 'new rigidity' coalesces the disparate pictures of young people so that a single moving picture appears before one's eyes.

On the basis of this single moving picture of ambitions, youth researchers have emphasised the commonality of experience among contemporary youth. Under the shadows of the individualisation thesis this is often characterised by weakening class effects. Woodman (2009) observes in this specific context the death of social class and questions whether the class-focused concepts of sociology are up to the task of theorising the contemporary world.

Since the main aim of this chapter is to critically consider this theoretical posture in relation to youth transitions in Kashmir, our first proposition is that despite the easier and more democratic access to education and more room for flexibility over one's life course than ever before, social inequality still persists and makes for differently perceived as well as real life transitions into adulthood. Secondly, we wish to test to what extent processes of making rational choices and decisions, which for Beck (1992) constitute individualisation, still require access to socio-economic and cultural resources.

As such resources are unequally distributed among social classes, they involve differential access to life chances and consequently lead to division of interest, preferences and orientation among young people in particular. Those who have more resources enjoy stable 'ontological security,'[5] have considerable advantages for negotiation of future risks and therefore have a 'post-reflexive choice'.[6] Contrarily, those, whose lower socio-economic status or class position remains the most stubborn and persistent factor in affecting their life-course trajectories, may find it harder to realise the desired

---

[5] According to Giddens (1991), in both pre-modern and modern traditional settings people acquired both a sense of social order, and of having a defined place in it, from the presence of established institutional hookson which to hang their selves and their identities. He calls this existential condition 'ontological security', the equanimity that comes from the conviction that your world is morally and socially ordered and your place in it is secure.

[6] Adams (2006:12) argues that in order to fully understand contemporary identity formation we also need to emphasise what comes after the movement of reflexive awareness, in which choices are resourced or otherwise.

self. As indicated above, such an analysis of engagements with particular socio-economic positions and attitudes towards the future was central to Bourdieu's theorising of social reproduction, which suggests that there is still a role for appropriate forms of class analysis.

Methodology

This chapter is based on empirical material, composed of survey interviews, carried out in three secondary schools in Srinagar city of Kashmir in April-August 2011. There were 100 survey respondents in the age group of 16-20 years and roughly equal numbers of interviews were conducted at three schools: Tyndale-Biscoe and Mallinson School (hereafter TBMS), Sri Pratap Singh Higher Secondary School (hereafter SPHS) and Kothibagh Girls' Higher Secondary School (hereafter KGHS). Because TBMS has the Tyndale-Biscoe boys' wing and the Mallinson girls' wing, respectively half of the interviews were conducted in these two wings. Respondents were chosen on the basis of random selection strategy and the interviews lasted for an hour to 1.5 hours. The study concerned a qualitative, cross-sectional design in which young people's views about their lived experience, future prospects, ambitions and impediments were elicited and compared. For data collection an interview guide was used. The objective of using this technique was primarily to give respondents maximum opportunity to reveal their world of experiences without imposing any limitations and predetermined alternatives.

After the collection of data, the transcripts were analysed using a qualitative content analysis. Texts were read and re-read in search of themes and sub-themes, covering the study's major propositions and objectives. The interview quotes and narratives relating to these themes were first categorised and then grouped separately on a school-wise basis. Later a comparative analysis was conducted on the data to develop conceptualisations of similarities and differences. The interview quotes in our analysis below reflect the actual transcript as closely as possible, though some stylistic changes were made to make the excerpts more readable. To protect confidentiality and anonymity, names of research participants have not been used throughout.

TBMS was founded in 1880 by Christian missionaries and still has affiliations with the 'Church Mission Society'. Currently it caters to children from lower kindergarten to class XII. As one of the best schools in Jammu & Kashmir in terms of infrastructure and excellence in education, it has a separate identity in the valley, with stupendous achievements over the years, producing doctors, lawyers, engineers and civil servants of Kashmir valley. Its students mostly have parents who are high-class business owners, doctors, upper-level managers and engineers. Therefore, TBMS students enjoy privileged economic and cultural capital, while SPHS and KGHS are government schools in the heart of Srinagar city, with students who are often mid-range in economic and cultural capital. Parents were mostly in service employment, lower level business owners or labourers and therefore in certain cases they approximate 'new cultural intermediaries' (Bourdieu, 1984). On the whole these three schools represent two socio-economically contrasting categories of youth that provided a fertile ground for the exploration of Bourdieu's notions of habitus in relation to future orientations and sense of possibilities and limitations, as well as reflexivity among young people.

Future Prospects and Ambitions

From the analysis of the accounts provided by these young people in interviews, we became attuned to the different life ambitions ranging from 'any job is fine' to becoming something specific, such as a secretary, professional cricketer, engineer, electrician, health technician, leader, Kashmir Administrative Service (KAS) officer, Indian Administrative Service (IAS) officer, surgeon, high-class business owner, social worker, professor or teacher. When asked what they wanted to be or what they planned or prepared to be, most of the interviewed students at SPHS and KGHS, however, did not or were not able to articulate any particular occupational career. They responded in diverse ways, such as: 'I don't know, I've not decided yet, I am only sixteen, not sure whether I'll be able to study further, I want a high-paid job', or repeating our question and laughing. Relatively, in the diverse voices of these youths, a sense of uncertainty and unpredictability was dominant. Very few named professional careers such as doctors, lawyers, engineers and professors. In certain cases SPHS and KGHS youth wanted to pursue somewhat vague and idealistic careers. For example, one male youth said he would like to be a professor of English and earn a lot of money. While he currently found it difficult to even understand spoken or written English, money was clearly the focus.

Comparatively, young people at TBMS, by and large from well-off and privileged families, usually desired occupational careers such as becoming an IAS officer, without stressing money or income attached to the position, and they were usually specific in stating their ambitions. Several explanations may be offered for these significant differences in responses. One seems to be a consequence of their respective lived experiences. For example SPHS and KGHS students' stress on money reflects their economic disadvantage and the often unrealistic approach towards the occupational field indicates some misfits in their life trajectories. In nearly all interviews at SPHS and KGHS, money and the familial financial situation were important issues. Their hope for mobility was rooted in realising material goals, reflected by citing people who earn good money without higher education and placing money as a top priority in life:

> You know my Mom has a saying 'study hard, study hard, you're smarter than this, you can be an engineer or something', and I think everyone wants to be a little different with good education and a prestigious job. But you know that I've seen the limits that my parents are confronted with. It is becoming difficult for them and would be

more so in future, because they are getting older, so how long they will manage for me, my sister and my brother . . . Nowadays even a university degree turns useless. So it is better to get engaged early with something that returns early and helps to develop material position. (SPHS 11th-grade male).

There are people around [neighbours], stable environment, you know. I want to own a shop and earn money instead of paying tuition. (SPHS 12th-grade male).

I will work as a nurse and if that is not possible, become a singer. That [singing] makes me happy. (KGHS 11th-grade female).

These concerns can be interpreted as the result of a complex and possibly compounding mix of social, cultural and economic disadvantage. It indicates the kind of habitus dislocation that has also been reported in other studies of working class students in higher education institutions (Aries and Seider, 2005; Lehmann, 2007). As noted, TBMS students envisioned exclusively professional careers and were usually quite specific. A 10th-grade female said: 'I want to become a social worker and start my own school for the marginalised children and youth of the society'. An 11th-grade female wanted to become a doctor and provide free healthcare facilities to poor and needy people. On the whole, the majority of TBMS students expressed and favoured professional occupations such as doctors, lawyers, IAS or KAS careers or business. In the narratives of some, a concern for others was reflected. For example:

> I would love to be a leader of Kashmir and do something to tackle this historical lingering issue once and for all. I've seen people dying and crying, which I think is the extreme thing for a human being to see. I really think that if this dream of mine comes true, I'd be the bravest person in the world. (TBMS 11th-grade male).

> I've planned to crack the IAS. My Mom and Dad want to see me in the administration of the state and it has now become my ambition to realise this end. (TBMS 12th-grade female).

Equally sports like cricket and academic fields were also named in the narratives of TBMS students. For example:

> I think I'd love to be a professional cricketer and play at national and international level, and want to travel across the world. (TBMS 10th-grade male).

> You know I really love writing poetry and prose, I've a dream to become a reputed personality the world over. (TBMS 11th-grade male).

In a nutshell these narratives suggest, at the very least, that habitus location still matters in a globalised world and makes for differences in the preferences, interests and attitudes of young people. TBMS students were aiming at the highest status and 'caring' occupational fields, and they displayed national and international level interests. On the other hand SPHS and KGHS youth, apart from economic disadvantage (their preoccupation with money may be interpreted as lack of economic capital), also displayed disadvantages related to cultural capital, such as their uncertainty about a professional career. Since habitus or living space instils a 'sense of one's place' (Bourdieu, 1984), we are attuned to a sense of these young people, drawing creatively from cultural forms to express themselves in ways that usually, but not always, conform to the characteristics of the larger class habitus to which they belong. Or they have internalised orientation to action inscribed in their demeanours, reflexes and movement (Bourdieu, 1977). Again in so far as class differences become inscribed in people's minds (Bourdieu, 1984) and convey a feeling for one's own possibilities and limitations, for example how one is likely to perform in school or work, objective external constraints are reinforced by perceptions. Standards of perception and evaluation to express preferences are mediated through the habitus as a form of embodied social, economic and cultural capital. As Bourdieu (1996: 2) held:

> While it is no doubt true that agents construct social reality and enter into struggles and transactions aimed at imposing their vision, they always do so

with points of view, interest, and principles of vision determined by the position they occupy in the very world they intend to transform or preserve.

The social mobility project thus has its roots in transformation of habitus. As Sayer (2005: 31) notes, 'habitus can be changed deliberately, at least in part, by repeated practices aimed at the embodiment of new dispositions'. We noticed such negotiations in the narratives of young people. For example:

I just love to become so independent, in a good way, have family, good salaried job, a car and enough wealth. That is my dream. (KGHS 11th-grade female).

I've got an idea to study hard, try MBBS. If I got success I'd travel to Saudi and settle there. I've heard it is good over there, if one is looking for enough money. (SPHS 11th-grade male).

I just want to get any job as early as possible, invest in business and do a couple of things that make quick money and have joys of life.(SPHS 12th-grade male).

I'll study hard, get a good earning job, give tuition, make huge wealth, have a car, a beautiful house, get married and enjoy life and be happy. (KGHS 11th-grade female).

These narratives provide the clues of what Beck-Gernsheim (1996) terms life as a 'planning project', or Gidden's (1991: 81) reflexive choice, a choice made with considerable deliberation beforehand, or Beck's (1992) 'do it yourself biographies'. But all this happens to be paradoxical, for the very reason that, in order to be of much use, planning requires a fairly predictable stable future (Adams, 2006) and reflexivity itself does not equate to choice to move beyond the parameters set by socio-economic location (Brannen and Nilsen, 2002). Dreams and ambitions are evident. Here again the relative preoccupation with acquiring money, material security or, to go back to previous quotes, feeling uncertain, as expressed by SPHS and KGHS youth, indicates the limiting effect of habitus mediated through socio-economic location. The ambition by a young male respondent, as cited above, to 'do a couple of things that make quick money', clearly indicates his feeling that he is probably going to pursue a relatively low-paid job, which he thinks is accessible rather than desirable, and will then need to do other things to promote his fantasy. A closer analysis of the accounts of TBMS students also displayed their penchant for money, but in a different way, reflecting their privileged backgrounds and an advantage for negotiation of future risks. For example:

> It feels like I only want to go for business studies and get stuff done. It is time you know? To do something that really matters nowadays, even if it requires paying as much money, and I want to

make my parents feel proud that I've done what I wanted to do and got to where I wanted, and that they [parents] would be happy for that. (TBMS 11th-grade male).

The dispositions and attitudes of TBMS students also displayed a self-disciplined and flexible approach to adapt to and deal with a future which they see to be constantly changing:

Knowledge is ever changing and so are the desirability and ambitions. I am so confused which lines to follow and where to start, because you know? I don't want to get stuck to a boring job. So I expect to try different things and get at where I really want to be and settle down what my aim is. (TBMS 10th-grade female).

Such a self-reflexive and flexibility-oriented discourse clearly confirms the TBMS students' confidence that they could master future challenges and are expectant rather than apprehensive. They believe that it is up to them what they make of the future. This was not the same among the SPHS and KGHS youth, whose typical singular concern focused on economic capital and material goals. However, this does not mean that SPHS and KGHS youth did not think in terms of a wide range of choices and opportunities, but they did so in the knowledge of their socio-economic status, which to a large extent has scheduled and standardised their life course trajectories so far. Here we agree with Goldthrope (1996: 484) that there are persistent 'macro-social regularities' in relationships between the class of origin and eventual educational and occupational outcomes. It may be because of these concerns that Goldthrope (1987) was firmly of the opinion that purely economic criteria had to be used in defining class situations, and these issues had to be distinguished from reputation and social standing that Weber (1978 [1920]: 302-7) had earlier called 'status situation'.

Perceived Challenges

This section deepens the analysis by studying the constraints and barriers that young people perceived for their future orientations and ambitions. These stemmed from their structural contexts, subjective orientations and personal resources. When asked what kinds of constraints they feel keep them off their goals and ambitions, almost all young people at each school expressed their concerns in this respect. However, most of their expressions suggested that young people are feckless or irresponsible and put themselves at risk through their own actions and cultural responses. Nevertheless, reviewing their narratives closely, we noticed that TBMS students were more prone to blaming themselves and their personal traits like disinterest, laziness or lack of ability, whereas the obstacles revealed in discussions with

SPHS and KGHS youth were each related in terms of needs, such as increased access to information, financial problems, more time for educational pursuits, language barriers and educational pitfalls. Though sometimes the students expressed subjective weaknesses, they were often compounded with concrete external objective constraints, for example paucity of money at home, trust deficit and weak cohesion, not knowing the right people at the right places, and lack of parental intervention in their educational pitfalls. These disadvantages are rooted in economic, social and cultural capital deficits, of which these young people seemed all too aware:

> It seems like everyone wants to do as good as anybody else. But when it comes on ground [socio-economic status], it is like hard to do what one wants. I know a lot of people, my locals, having good amount of money behind them, paying for private coaching, doing language courses [English] and admitted to academically top ranking schools. They just live with [advantage] all their life and it's normal for them, and at times it's like 'oh God' I wish it were that easy! But at the end of the day it [socio-economic advantage/disadvantage] has always been relevant and I feel excluded and frustrated. (SPHS 11th-grade male).

Limited or lack of English proficiency, affecting school work, academic success and other spheres like training and jobs, was also articulated and recognised by the SPHS and KGHS youth. For example:

I think it's a lot easier to get stuff done if one has proficiency in the English language. Its deficiency disturbs me in my studies. Many times I can't understand what the teacher is talking about. Last time I asked my father for some money, so that I could attend a language course at a private institution, but he couldn't manage that. He is working as a labourer in a cement factory. (SPHS 11th-grade male).

It [English language] is extremely important and demanded skill to have today and is useful, whenever you apply for a job or even computer literacy requires English. But it needs supportive context like parents must be educated. Look, my parents have probably studied up to middle, how come they would be helpful when it comes to learning English or other subjects like maths or science? So these inadequacies added by monetary limits hamper our pathways. (KGHS 12th-grade female).

You know? My biggest hurdle is [stressed by interviewee] not having extra direction, like how to prepare and how to do maximum in exams. I'm a bit struggling with maths and science, otherwise I am so anxious to do my best, because my Mummy and Daddy do somehow manage for me and I think it is a big responsibility for me to do something for them. They don't know personally any teacher here, who could have been supportive, as I see teachers showing some extra attention towards some students. Might be their parents have some relation with them [teachers]. (KGHS10th-grade female).

At first sight, these narratives recall what Annette Kuhn (1995: 98) describes as class being 'something beneath your clothes, under your skin, in your reflexes, in your psyche, in the very core of your being'. The reliance on cultural and social capital beyond economic assets as specifically expressed by SPHS and KGHS youth in the above narratives leaves open the relative contributions of specific forms of capital. However, simultaneously it confirms that those lower in economic capital also lack in social and cultural capital. For example the statement '. . . couldn't attend language course . . . father couldn't manage . . . 'presented in one of the narratives above indicates that lack of economic capital leads to a lack of relevant skills, cultural capital. Because social capital is located in networks, it is therefore 'relatively irreducible to the economic and cultural capital . . . [of] a given agent' (Bourdieu, 2004: 21). Yet as Bourdieu (1986) reminded us, access to economic capital is the most effective route to acquiring cultural and social capital. Economically privileged individuals have the financial resources to fund the development of cultural capital, and they can use their privileged position to create social capital. The statements '. . . and that I feel excluded and frustrated . . .' and '. . . don't know personally any teacher . . . supportive . . .' clearly exemplify how low economic capital leads to weak cohesion, low social growth and consequently weak social capital. This implies that situating social capital in its interrelations with other capital is necessary given the persistently differential outcomes associated with disadvantage and privilege (Bottrell, 2009: 481).

Together these narratives accentuate a complementary relationship between all three types of capital. However, as indicated, economic capital and social capital, the 'bridging variety' (Putnam, 2000) are important, mainly by creating access to cultural capital. This conceptualisation of interdependent forms of capital (Bourdieu, 2004) clearly allows a better understanding of these disadvantaged young people. Although SPHS and KGHS youth signalled their sense of constraint by external structures, which do not lie within their personal capacity to transform and reconstruct, they seem to reflexively engage with the reality of disadvantage. However, this reflexivity or recognition of itself functions also as a mechanism for social marginalisation in specific contexts of school and community, and arguably constitutes and compounds adversities faced by disadvantaged young people. For example, a youth with a high awareness of belonging to the working class may have more negative outcome expectations for taking actions to develop artistic skills than a youth who is less aware of his/her social class.

This was not the concern among TBMS youth who typically, as given in the examples cited above, mostly named obstacles arising from their subjective orientations, such as poor work ethics, disinterest, lack of ability or loss of motivation. Their accounts point to a crucial role for parental and familial resources, while they think that they have the power to shape and control the future. They never talked about structural constraints; rather they regularly indicated that constraints arose because of their own lack of ability to beat future odds:

> I feel I've every sort of facility available, so comfortable. My Mom and Dad give me everything I require [. . .] I mean I'm being so looked after and I think that if I won't do something good for myself, that would be all because of my own lack of ability to concentrate, because I usually spend so much time in gossip and watching television. Still no need to worry, I'll just draw from my parents for a little longer till I actually settle down. (TBMS 11th-grade female).

I don't need to do much to get along [. . .] my parents give me each and everything so that I could flourish academically. They frequently approach my teachers, pay for tuition, and you know my Mummy is always like study, study, study . . . [laughs], so motivating myself to work for myself, but sometimes I just feel bored, and want to be free to do what I want. So I think it would be my own laziness or disinterest, if I won't do anything good in my future. (TBMS 11th-grade male).

Yet, these excerpts of individualisation narratives were constructed and situated, both explicitly and implicitly, from within their respective class habitus. As these quotes suggest, TBMS students were quite self-reflexive about their relative privilege. It was perhaps this sense of privilege that works as a source of constraint that these young people may otherwise feel to come from their individual traits. For example, having lots of money to shop and party, and less to do, and absence of first-hand experience in the 'real world of work' might have created certain moral disadvantages, like lack of work ethic and responsibility taking:

Oh! Exactly experimenting is the most important to see what you want, to create your way by yourself, inventing things for yourself and realising desires. But being on benefits, I mean having easy access to things like sports kit, pocket money . . .

[laughs], I sometimes lose sight of my personal goals and I'm afraid to set goals, but most of all afraid to fail.(TBMS 11-th grade male).

These youths also seemed to assume that their parental economic, cultural and social resources would bring them success, so that personal failing would not let them down. This again pointed towards the importance of parental resources for young people to feel comfortable with the reflexive self-discipline apparently required for success. Additionally, these quotes again confirm, at least for the cohort we investigated, that whenever interpersonal and communal social ties are exploited for the accumulation and exchange of economic and cultural capital (Bourdieu, 1986) as well as human capital (Becker, 1964), social capital is also at work (Coleman, 1988). The statement '. . . they frequently approach my teachers . . .' as given in one of the above quotes, indicates that parents with economic and cultural capital often proceed from a distinct class-based sense of entitlement, using a strategy of 'concrete cultivation' (Lareau, 2003) to influence the school personnel on behalf of their children. In exercising this strategy, parents aim at directly facilitating their children's educational and social growth through strategic institutional interventions.

SPHS and KGHS youths, on the other hand, instantly spoke of the limitations placed upon them and their parents by their lower socio-economic status. Although they do have some economic and cultural capital, this is insufficient to counter the structured effects or it is fragmented and thus ineffective in strengthening collective efficacy and well-being. Consequently it gives rise to a vicious circle of low trust and weak cohesion. Nonetheless SPHS and KGHS youth were in no sense 'reflexivity losers' (Lash, 1994: 120) and can hardly be described as having no objective understanding of their social context. They had a productive sense of the tangible constraints they face, and some of them were looking at education as a route towards improved material and social circumstances. Here, our evidence adds to the body of thought that while there is reflexivity in the habitus of youth at the lower rungs of social structure, they lose out 'in relation to reflexivity'(Adams, 2006: 523), because they are marginalised by a social structure which empowers reflexivity in others.

Conclusions and Discussion

In conclusion this debate and discussion confirms that the life course and structural features of young people's lives are relevant to the production of very different types of orientation to the future. One may summarise this by saying simply that different socio-economic status of young people still shapes, in profound ways, their perceptions on life chances. It falsifies the assertion that amidst the many aspects of contemporary social change and the wide-ranging commentaries on these, the structural context can be simply described as de-traditionalised, involving a process of 'liberation', in which traditional ways of life can no longer be counted on and are irrelevant.

In many respects these theoretical positions give an impression that young people world-wide share the same challenges, interests and concerns, remark on how the world is shrinking and emphasise the commonality of experience of young people as economic systems begin melding. However, scrutinising the experience of young people in Kashmir, upon closer inspection, it is marked that structural context or more precisely the underlying social class-based inequalities still persist as a crucial structural feature of contemporary societies, shaping young people's life-chances and perceptions on the future.

Drawing on the conceptualisation of interdependent forms of capital (Bourdieu, 2004) our study refutes western-centric accounts of individualisation and their claims of irrelevance of social class in the understanding of the experiences of young people. Our major data examples support the proposition that making rational choices and decisions, which does constitute individualisation (Beck, 1992; Giddens, 1991) still requires access to socio-economic and cultural resources and/or is heavily dependent on one's class position. There were many pointers in our data that those higher in economic and cultural capital were more relaxed and comfortable with the reflexive self-discipline apparently required for success. While SPHS and KGHS youths tactically or directly acknowledged economic disadvantage, they also conceived impediments to their prospects which were structural in nature. TBMS youths, on the other hand, presented ambitions which were much less material, and the future was something to be negotiated by management or reflexivity. Moreover, the constraints they nominated, though structural from our point of view, were subjective in their perspectives. They had a feeling of considerable advantage for negotiation of future risks and the maintenance of a stable 'ontological security' (see Giddens, 1991: 35-69). This was less so for disadvantaged SPHS and KGHS youths, whose future was preoccupied with material goals, displaying their lack of ontological security and strategic risk taking. Hence, this again supports the proposition that reflexivity is mediated through habitus as a form of class-based embodied economic, social and cultural capital.

Indeed, it is through reflexivity that SPHS and KGHS youth perceived a dearth of social opportunities and life-chances for themselves, which in turn had important ramifications for levels of self-esteem and future aspirations. Social change, thus, may be facilitating a reflexivity which infiltrates the fog of structured dispositions. Sweetman (2003) asserts that reflexivity has become a general capability reflecting social change, embracing more and more areas of life including our sense of identity. But identities are still fashioned in the fitness to translate the choices which emerge from this complex interplay into meaningful realities. Even a heavily qualified reflexivity can only tell a partial story of contemporary identity (Adams, 2006).

The arguments in this chapter, however, negate accounts which stress the efficacy of cultural capital in the inter-generational transmission of privilege and disadvantage (e.g. Threadgold and Nilan, 2009). Our data examples suggest that economic and social capital can still also be highly important, particularly by creating access to crucial cultural capital. Simply, if access to education is widened, economically well-off families can gather their children in academically selective schools, and pay extra for tuition and language courses, as our data indicated, thereby giving their wards access to a broader curriculum. Further, by using distinct class-based strategic institutional interventions to influence school personnel on behalf of their children, advantaged families aim at directly facilitating their children's educational and social growth. Such insights need to be aware of what constitutes sociology as a plural field of study and research. If we address ourselves only to one-dimensional empirical reality and do not listen to the underlying 'silent narratives', we are indeed ignoring a key sociological resource, 'the sociological imagination' (Brannen and Nilsen, 2005: 426).

Altogether our evidence suggests that continuing class or habitus-based transmission of advantages or disadvantages cannot simply be ignored or its casual consequences denied as some proponents of the reflexive modernisation and individualisation thesis suggest. Rather, at least in the Indian context, social class not only remains important, but is emerging as a useful concept in sociological analysis. It is a stubborn and persistent factor affecting educational attainments and occupational destinations of young people. This is reflected in the argument by Reay (2005: 924) that class is 'deeply embedded in every day interaction and institutional processes, in the struggle for identity and recognition, whether it is acknowledged or not'.

Taken together, the characterisation of this debate reflects well what Brannen and Nilsen (2002) suggest that the way young people behold their futures must be looked at through the lens of the dual epistemology of agency and structure. This debate strongly connects with Bourdieu's arguments and brings out that the life-course and structural features of young people's lives remain relevant to the production of very different types of orientation to the future. Social backgrounds still provide the resources necessary to think and manage, and continue to shape young people's experiences and their perceptions on life-chances in profound ways.

Hence, we argue here that the key question in youth research, both methodologically and theoretically, should still be about with whom, where and how young people negotiate their life-trajectories. Youth transitions should be sited and grasped in terms of a network of relationships, typically inter-generational, with family and social class as major institutions, as they equip young people with pertinent resources to actualise whatever choices they may aspire to.

Finally, the Euro-American-centric representations of young people, which instantly formulate youth with change, the 'autonomous individual' or the 'sovereign subject,' as if they were per se the carriers of innovation, living in no man's land, are trivialities that should be instantly reproached and refuted. To do this, Lagree (2004) argues that sociologists would have to move out of their backyard, so to speak the 'nation state'. In doing so, comparative methodology seems to be the most powerful analytical tool for describing local contexts and obtaining a more generalised and universal view of ongoing transformations.

5

Youth and Globalisation in India and China: A Study of Mental Health

At the beginning of a new millennium, globalisation is a central driving force behind the rapid social, political and economic changes that are reshaping modern societies and world order (Giddens, 1990; Castells, 1996). This process is changing the character of human interaction in many spheres like social, cultural, environmental and technological and is changing the way we perceive time and space, and the way we think about the world and ourselves (Kunitz, 2000; Lee, 2000).

The discourses that are contiguous to this 'brave new world' of globalisation (Bhugra and Mastrogianni 2004:10) suggest different philosophical and ideological perspectives (e.g. hyperglobalisers, sceptics and transformationalists) which have led to somewhat antagonistic standpoints about the globalisation and its bearing on individuals and societies. However, alongside this debate it is largely agreed that globalisation has become a controversial topic. Its power and influence on the world order bring opportunities for some people and pose threats to others (McMichael and Beaglehole, 2000). The utmost disparities reinforced by globalisation are a lot to be found within the margins of nation-states, rather than between underdeveloped and developed countries (Bhugra and Mastrogianni, 2004: 10-20). It is likely to escalate social inequality by aggravating differences in access to and distribution of resources (Stiglitz, 2002). George (1998) and Castles (2004) postulate that globalisation leads inevitably to the decline of the welfare state through the vetoing of investment towards greater social expenditure and full employment by international financial markets. Because, poverty, economic disparity, underdevelopment and mental health are co-related (Desjarlais, Eisenberg and Good, *et al.*, 1995; Bibeau, 1997), it is hardly surprising then that globalisation and its related social and economic changes affect the mental health of individuals and societies.

Albeit, it is challenging to envisage the impact of globalisation on the incidence and course of psychiatric disorders, what is conversely true is that mental disorders can no longer be separated from the global milieu that shapes our lives. The social processes allied with globalisation, such as employment pressures, migration, poverty, culture, and social change can be risk or protective factors for disorders such as suicide, substance abuse, antisocial behaviour, anxiety and depression. Globalisation also has effects on the specification of health and social care to those with mental health problems, whether or not these have been fabricated by globalisation (Manning and Patel, 2008: 299-300). According to Kirmayer and Minas (2000) globalisation encroaches on psychiatry in three main ways: through its effect on the forms of individual and collective identity, through the impact of economic inequalities on mental health, and through the shaping and propagation of psychiatric knowledge itself.

These multifaceted associations between globalisation, health and social and mental health are only now started to be investigated, and scholars highlight the need for a clearly defined research and policy arrangements to respond to the challenges posed (Lee, 2000). Specifically for the age cohort 15—35 years, there is paucity of literature on the association between globalisation and mental health. Since youth stand at the centre of this panorama of change, those youth who do not hold the aptitude and capability to espouse the gauntlet of competition are left out. To a certain degree, this has increased the alienation, affecting the mental and social health of a substantial portion of the youth population particularly in developing countries. However, for the most part mental health consequences of globalisation for youth remain undervalued and uncounted.

Affects of globalisation on mental health of young people are imperative to be concerned about in the light of the substantial and increasing burden of disease attributable to mental illness (Lopez, Mathers, Ezzati, Jamison and

Murray, 2006; Prince, Patel, Saxena and Rahman, *et. al.,* 2007). According to World Health Organisation (WHO) estimates for the year 1999, neuropsychiatric disorders and suicide amount to 12.7 percent of the global burden of disease (GBD) and related conditions. Specifically suicide is among the top three causes of death of young people aged 15—35 (WHO, 2000) and is one of the leading causes of death of young women in India and China (Wortley, 2000). The WHO (2003) report indicates that by the year 2020, adolescent psychiatric disorders will increase by more than 50 percent to become one of the five leading causes of disability among adolescents. The most common mental disorders affecting adolescents and young people worldwide is depression, predicted to be the leading single cause of disease burden globally by 2030. Yet currently 31 percent of countries do not have a specific public budget for mental health (Saxena, Thornicroft, Knapp, Whiteford, *et al.,* 2007), 40 percent of countries have no mental health policies and more than two-thirds of the world's population (68 percent), the majority of whom are in Africa and South Asia, have access to only 0.04 psychiatrists per 100,000 of the population (WHO, 2005a).

Why India and China?

We base our exploration and analysis on data from two countries in South Asia—India and China—for three reasons. First, in the current literature on economic development we persistently come upon the concept of 'demographic dividend' which empirically refers to the rise in the rate of economic growth, due to increase in the share of working—age (15—59 years) people in a population. Since India and China accounts for more than a fifth of youth population in the developing world (Lloyd, Behrman, Stromquist and Cohen, 2006), this dividend is projected essentially to accrue to these two countries.

However, there is no gainsaying that population is more than mere numbers. It is the quality of young people that will decide the level to which India and China can garner this 'demographic gift'. Unsurprisingly it brings to the forefront issues allied not only to the increasing demand for labour, nature of the labour force, its employability, the quantity, quality and relevance of education, but also presumes that the desired quality of the population bulge entering the workforce in terms of health must be ensured. Particularly their mental well-being is all crucial or else the potential of dividend would turn out to be a burden, a problematic too.

Secondly, in the evolution of the world economy particularly during last two decades, India and China are measured as the leading economies in transition in the global economy. However, along with the globalisation of economy, these two countries in South Asia turned out to be home to a large number of people from countries with varying cultures, political systems and levels of social development. Consequently, on the one hand there have been massive changes in the social, cultural and political structures of these two countries, which in a sense resulted into tremendous rise in the level of aspirations of people, but the material and institutional means for their fulfilment could not be evolved rapidly. On the other privatisation, vetoing of welfare certificates and social expenditure due to global pressures, and altered economic growth can further add to this stress and contributes to mental health problems (Bhavsar and Bhugra, 2008: 379). Particularly young people may be more susceptible to stress from growing up within this milieu of cultural multiplicity and uncertainty.

Thirdly, there is a need to fill in a gap in the literature on mental health of youth with regard to globalisation in India and China.

Methodology

Our data come from epidemiological studies, Psych-INFO, WHO, ILO and Pub-Med, Academic Search Premier, Google Scholar and general academic literature; covering the socio-structural determinants of mental health and globalisation and health in general. Subsequent to intensive reviews and summarisation, the crucial outcomes of globalisation that may possibly impact on mental health of youth were documented, and the best accessible data on each theme was obtained. The socio—economic risk factors recognised, included poverty and social inequality, increased educational competition and consequent pressure, and unemployment, underemployment and work stress. There were other risk factors like 'urbanisation,' 'trade in neurotoxic', 'globalisation as an acculturative stressor,' 'identity shifts and mental health' etc. However, as it was not feasible to cover all these topics, we conducted a systematic review of already three mentioned topics.

Recent sociologies of youth frequently emphasize the four interlinked themes regarding young people's lives: social class, poverty, education and school to work transition (Jeffrey, 2003). The interaction between these variables is described as a vicious cycle in which the conditions of poverty lead to low education, social exclusion, reduced access to health services, malnutrition and increased risk of violence, and thereby increased prevalence of and worse outcomes for mental disorders (Patel, 2001). Indeed in a modern 'educational world,' the relation between poverty, education, psychological well being, and youth development is, of course, debated in many different scientific contexts and from numerous perspectives, which articulate youth life and educational life as two parallel and interacting pathways of youth development (See Morch, 2003; Winefield, 2002).

Given this, the poverty and social inequality, increased educational competition and consequent pressure, and unemployment, underemployment and work stress as themes of our review and analysis seems to be more appropriate, and more directly linked with the lives of youth.

The definition of mental health problem was constructed in a broader way to cover schizophrenia and other non-affective psychotic disorders, major depression, dysthymia, bipolar disorder, generalised anxiety disorder (GAD), panic disorder, obsessive-compulsive disorder (OCD) and all kinds of worries, anxiety and frustration.

The literature we reviewed used different age brackets (e.g. 10-19, 15-24 years). However, in depth reviews, where possible further widened the age range to 10—35 years for the purposes of reporting maximum data. Nevertheless, the majority of cases in the overall analysis fell between 15 to 35 years of age range. Owing to the dearth of empirical data directly relating globalisation and mental health of youth, this study by logicality adopts an exploratory approach. The analysis therefore, looks into the impact of globalization on identified socio—economic determinants of mental health and thereby exemplifies how globalisation can be projected to impact on mental health of youth in India and China. Such analyses also entail an approach to the sociology of knowledge as specifically developed in the writings of C. Wright Mills (1959). His point being that:

> The sociological imagination involves the ability to comprehend the relationship between history and biography. Only through analyzing the connection between the two can 'private troubles' be seen in terms of 'public issues,' making sociology relevant in the sense that individual lives can be understood in the context of contemporary society as well as history. This involves a processional approach to the agency—structure problematic whereby its dynamic nature is captured. One side of the dynamic cannot be understood without reference to the other (Brannen and Nilsen, 2005: 422).

Results and Discussion
Poverty and Widening Social Inequality

Most advocates of liberalisation and globalisation insist that the distributive impact of globalisation is largely neutral (e.g. Dollar, 2001) and income inequality within countries has remained by and large stable over the last few decades (Li, Squire, and Zou, 1998). Specifically the two instances typically cited as evidences of the advantages of globalisation are India and China (Corrigall, Plagerson, Lund and Myers, 2008). However recently there is a considerable volume of research that challenges these assertions and argues that economic growth is frequently accompanied by widening socio—economic inequalities (George, 2002). Katz (2000) suggests that the deregulation of labour markets has played a role in increasing income inequality within nations. Similarly Kelly (2003) proposes that:

> Market deregulation favours the dominant, strong economies of the West and fails to offer developing countries an opportunity to strengthen their infrastructure sufficiently to compete in a global economy. Globalisation, by this logic, will lead to further poverty, inequality and social injustice (p. 465).

Such experiences are not missing in the post-reform India and China, where despite current annual GDP growth rates at 7 percent and 8.9 percent respectively (Humphrey, 2006), economic and social inequality is increasing. Social inequality in China has increased dramatically since the adoption of a 'free market' economy. In the early 1980s, the richest 10 percent of the population earned less than 20 percent of national income. By 1995, they earned 33.7 percent while the bottom 10 percent accounted for only 1.87 percent (Khan and Carl, *et al.,* 2001). By 2005 the top 10 percent earned 45 percent of the income, while the bottom 10 percent earned only 1.4 percent. Particularly in rural China 42 percent of households experienced a decreased income in absolute terms from 2000 to 2002 (Gilboy, George and Eric Heginbotham, 2004). Between 1980 and 2005, the 'Gini ratio' measure of inequality in China indicates a growing gap from 0.2 considered acceptable to 0.45 signifying serious polarisation and increasing social unrest (Wang, 2005).

Likewise in India there are strong evidences to suggest that inequality, measured by the coefficient of variation in per capita SDP across the major states, has nearly doubled since 1970-71, i.e. from about 0.2 to 0.4. However, more drastically the discrepancy in per capita income has widened sharply since 1986-87 (Nagaraj, Varoudakis and Veganzones, 2000; Kurian 2007). In absolute terms the distribution of income ratio, which improved in favour of rural India between 1970-71 and 1980-81 declined relative to urban per capita income, from 42 per cent in 1980-81 to 38 per cent in 1993-94 (Raj, 1990; Nagaraj, 2000; Bardhan, 2009). At household or individual level this inequality is evident, not only in income terms, but also in terms of health, access to education and other services. Evidences for rising inequality in India over the past two decades are also set out in Jha (2000) and Deaton (2002) who agree that inequality in India has been increasing in recent years, and consumption by the poor did not rise as fast as average consumption.

One can use much of this evidence to argue that globalisation has resulted in an increase in social inequality. However, the impact of social inequalities on the mental health is contested and we are unable to control for the impact of other social factors. Yet it is likely on the basis of this evidence that levels of social inequality do have a lot of effect on the mental health, particularly of young people, because in this context it is likely that:

> Globalisation for some means localisation for others. Being local may be seen as a sign of backwardness, whereas being global may be a sign of modernity. An integral part of the globalising process is progressive spatial segregation, separation and exclusion. This, combined with a sense of alienation, can be seen as a cumulative way of increasing the stress of vulnerable individuals. It is possible that with such processes of globalisation, cultures may be denuded of their psychologically protective effects (Bhurga, *et al.,* 2004: 10-12).

Poverty and social inequality therefore, is more than low-income or low consumption. It encompasses non-monetary aspects such as social exclusion, social vulnerability, and denial of opportunities and choice (Saxena, 2007: 883). Consistent with WHO (2009) report on *Mental Health, Poverty and Development*, people with the lowest socio-economic status (SES) have eight times greater relative risk for schizophrenia than those of the highest SES, and four times more likely to be unemployed or partly employed. Scholars have described the interaction of poverty and mental ill health as a vicious cycle in which the conditions of poverty lead to high levels of stress, social exclusion, reduced access to health services, malnutrition and increased risk of violence, and thereby increased prevalence of and worse outcomes for mental disorders (Patel, 2001). Consider the largest concentrations of young people living on less than US$ 1 a day are found in India 67.7 million and China 33.3 million (UN, 2005). Simultaneously the highest rates of suicide are found in India and China (WHO, 2004). In India more than 65 percent of all suicides occur in persons below 35 years of age with 35 percent in the age group of 15—24 years (NCRB, 2007), and nearly 90 percent of those who completed suicide belonged to the lower and lower middle socio—economic strata's (Gururaj and Isaac, 2001; 2004). Likewise Katageri (2010) in his study in Bangalore identified 59.4 percent of suicide victims (aged 15—24 years) were belonging to lower socio-economic status followed by middle class 36.1 percent, while 56.4 percent were financially dependent. Speaking generally, the number of suicides in India between 1995 and 2005, a decade in post reform period, has recorded an increase of 27.7 percent and 35.3 percent of suicide victims were youths of 15—29 years of age (NCRB, 2005).

Similarly in China among young adults 15—34 years of age, suicide has been the leading cause of death, accounting for 19 percent of all deaths. However, in rural China suicide rates were three times higher than urban rates—a difference that remained true for both sexes, for all age-groups, and over time (Phillips, Yang, Zhang, Wang, Ji, and Zhou, 2002b). Reports of suicides in the Chinese press and case studies conducted by various scholars and agencies suggest that the high rates of suicide currently experienced are related to the social change (including the rising prevalence of major economic losses for individuals, increased costs of health care, migration to urban areas for temporary or seasonal work, weakened family ties) and consequent widening inequalities that have occurred with the economic reforms which started in 1978 (Phillips, Liu, Huaqing and Zhang, 1999: 25-50). In this respect Patel and Kleinman (2003) postulate that hopelessness associated with poverty was a core experience of young women in rural China who had committed suicide and the survivors of suicide attempts. Another possible explanation for this phenomenon in China is the large numbers of persons with depressive illness due to social factors like poverty, who remain untreated (Phillips *et al.,* 1999). Zhang, Xiao, Shuiyuan and Zhou (2010) observed an additive interaction between lower level of social support, mental illness and suicide among young rural Chinese.

General speaking research reports indicate that psychiatric disorders have been consistently more common among people in lower social classes, and over 90 percent of those who commit suicide suffer from a diagnosable psychiatric disorder (Bertolote and Fleischmann, 2002). A review of epidemiological research in low and middle income countries (LMICs) has shown a very strong relationship between many indicators of poverty and common mental disorders. Rates for common mental disorders are about twice as frequent among the poor compared to the rich in Brazil, Chile, India and China (Patel, Araya, De-Lima, Ludermir, and Todd, 1999). Indeed, preliminary analysis of WHO *World Health Survey* data indicates that greater income inequality at a national level is associated with higher prevalence of mental illness (Pickett and Pearl, 2006).

Increased Educational Competition and Consequent Pressures

The combination of economic restructuring in the world economy and the powerful ideological conception of how educational delivery needs to be changed, spread by international institutions as consequences of the process of globalisation, is having a significant impact on educational systems worldwide (Carnoy and Rhoten, 2002). On the one hand it is the quantity and quality of education and training, which determine whether and how countries can participate in the processes of globalisation, such as global value chains, fragmentation, increased trade in final products, and migration. The quality of national educational systems is increasingly being compared internationally, which places increased emphasis on professional and technical courses, standards, testing, and on meeting standards by changing the way education is delivered. Simultaneously on the other hand globalisation pressurises most countries to reduce the growth of public spending on education, and to find alternative sources of funding for the expected expansion of their educational systems (see Carnoy, 2002). Consequently the most visible changes in the provision of education are the rise in private formal schooling and the increasing share of school costs (including the costs of the growing practice of supplementary tutoring) paid by parents. Classrooms moved away from a focus on egalitarianism and class struggle, instead emphasizing quality, competition, individual talents, and the mastery of concepts and skills important in the lobour market and development of science and technology (Broaded, 1983; Kwong, 1985; Lin, 1993).

Given this interaction, the dialectic between youth development and educational systems is important to study, not only in the way educational systems influence youth development but also in the way youth development demands changes in educational planning, contexts and methods. Some analysts go so far to argue that the rapid spread of formal education in the developing world is an important social trend affecting the health environment of adolescents and youth. Indeed academic learning is currently among the most important sources of stress faced by young people worldwide and Asian students in particular often have high academic burden, low satisfaction regarding their academic performance and strong external pressure to study, and may suffer more academic stress than their counterparts in Western countries (Dunne, Sun, and Nguyen, *et al.,* 2010).

This is possibly for the reasons that, since economic pressures on young people and parents in developing countries have become more intense, notions of what constitutes education and an educated person have become an increasingly important focus for processes of identity formation and social conflict (Jeffrey and Mecdowell, 2004). For example China's students today are preoccupied with money and power. Bill Gates has emerged as the most popular role model for them—a sharp contrast with the youth of the 1980s, many of whom wanted to be China's Einstein or Mother Teresa (Yan, 2006: 257). Secondly with increased growth in the youth population, rising aspirations due to foreign cultural contacts and correspondingly limited opportunities for admission in schools and colleges, particularly in professional courses, youth are under great pressure to perform. For example in 2006 a record 9.5 million students took China's college entrance exams, while colleges and universities could enroll only 2.6 million of students (Yan, 2006: 257). Parents often place a lot of pressure on their children to study hard, get good marks, succeed academically and honour family. Because, strong family centered traditions in China remain intact and family honor remains a crucial motivation to young people in their educational studies, career choices and social pursuits (Brown and Sarswathi, *et al.,* 2002). Studies also indicate that Chinese parents traditionally tend to be more controlling of their children compared to Western parents (Chao, 1994; Chao and Sue, 1996). This traditional parenting style has become more intensified and reinforced in the present global milieu, characterised by risk and uncertainty. Under such Creolisation (Bibeau, 1997) of local (parental deep concern for their children's future and family honour) and global pressures, adolescents and youth experience high levels of stress and anxiety. For example, the Research Centre of Chinese Youth conducted a nationwide survey (2005) among middle and high schools and found 57 percent of the students categorised their lives as unhappy because of the pressures of study, while 42 percent considered having good test scores the happiest thing in their lives. Chinese government has recently estimated that approximately 30 million adolescents aged 17 and under experience depression symptoms or other behavioral problems (Yip, 2006). Li and Zhu (2005) studied the mental health of private high school students in the Hunan province (central China) and reported that private high school students had a significantly higher score on eight items: compulsion, interpersonal sensitivity, depression, anxiety, hostility, fear, paranoid ideation and psychosis. One explanation was, parents had paid more money for their children to go to private schools and they expected higher scores from their children. If children cannot meet their parents' expectations to achieve academically, they may become fearful and anxious. A 2004 survey of 1,010 college students in central China reveals that 11 percent had thought of committing suicide. Likewise a 2005 survey of 200 students in a Beijing college found 30 percent had the idea of committing suicide (Yan, 2006: 259). Radio Free Asia, a free press agency in East Asia, attributes these symptoms to increased stress and pressure to succeed that children experience at school and at home (Radio Free Asia, 2004). Li and Prevatt (2008) found Chinese high school students were to report higher levels of fears and related anxieties than their Western counterparts. Ding, *et al.,* (1998) on the analysis of a questionnaire test among 2009 young students in Beijing and Hong Kong found disturbances caused by mental stress existed commonly among youth in these two cities. The main stimuli of these mental pressures were examination, study, personal future, family and money.

It is possibly because of such high expectations and pressures that according to the research by the China Youth and Children Research Association, anxiety disorders among college students increased by 8 percent between 1992 and 2005 and depression rose by 7 percent (Yinggi, 2010). Review of literature Indicates that such pressures to succeed academically are intense in the Indian context as well and Indian families too have high [educational] expectations of the individual (Deb, 2001; Bhurga *et al.,* 2004). However, traditionally it comes into view somewhat less significant compared to China. Nonetheless currently increases in secondary enrollment rates in India reflect emerging middle class parental desires and expectations (Kingdon, 2007). It is particularly at secondary and senior secondary school level when educational competition intensifies. Because, performances in these examinations is the main determining criteria for future admission to a high quality colleges and universities and admission to courses like medicine, engineering and management, parents urge their children to perform well and to this end tutors are called in and parents take time off to coach their children through exams. Memory pills' are devoured, nutritionists are consulted for the best brain food and newspapers devote sections to tackling exams. According to HSBC survey of 2500 Asian affluent's, 93 percent Mumbai (India) elite cited one of the major parameters of happiness as the ability to 'send children to the best schools and colleges abroad' (Times of India, 2007).

It is possibly because of these all pervasive competitions and parental expectations that a national study (2008) identified depression, anxiety and stress (DAS) significantly higher in the secondary and senior secondary classes. The scores in the three domains—depression, anxiety and stress were found to be remarkably correlated (Sanjiv, Bhasin, Sharma and Saini, 2010). Correspondingly DeSouza, Kumar and Shastri (2009) bring forth that 29 and 24 percent of Indian youth have high and very high aspirations respectively. Alongside, the study shows that 18 and 50 percent of Indian youth have high and very high levels of anxiety. Thus, higher the level of aspiration, greater the level of anxiety, however, the zones of anxiety that the Indian youth fell into were found influenced largely by SES and education. Nine out of every ten Indian youth who have very high aspirations feel that gaining access to higher education is extremely important (p. 100-10). Failing to rise up to that aspirations and expectations or are in process of meeting them, adolescents and youth suffer from frustration, aggression, undesirable complexes and depression. For example Ghaderi, Venkatesh, and Sampath (2009) compared the experiences of stress, anxiety and depression among the Indian and the Iranian students studying in different departments of university of Mysore, and identified the DAS level of Indian students was significantly higher than those of Iranian students. Financial pressures and concern with grades, examination and results were major stressors among Indian students. Likewise Deb, Chatterjee, and Kerryann (2010) in a study in Eastern India identified 38 percent adolescent aged between 13—17 suffering from high anxiety. Singh, Lal and Shekhar (2010) in a study of 381 medical college students (MBBS) in Northern India found half (49.1percent) of the students had symptoms of depression. On examining the influence of school demands on the daily time use and subjective states of Indian young people, Verma, Sharma and Larson (2002) postulate that school work generated negative subjective states as reflected in low affect state, below-average activation levels, lower feeling of choice, and higher social anxiety. Most of the students were found to spend one third of their waking time in school—related activities.

It is again relevant to mention here that in India more adolescents die of suicide than AIDS, cancer, heart disease, obesity, birth defects and lung disease. Among the specified causes of suicide failure in examinations is the predominant (NCRB, 2002). In 2006-07, a record 5,857 students took their own life compared to 800 in 1998—99, which works out to a stunning 16 suicides a day (NCRB, 2007). Katageri (2010) in his study in Bangalore identified that majority of suicide victims (aged 15—24 years) were students and failure in examinations was one of the main causes. As per the reports from Child and Adolescent Psychiatry Clinic, AIIMS diagnosis of adolescent depression in India has gone up from 0.4 percent in 1980 to 6.5 per cent in 2005 (Datta, 2008).

Unemployment, Underemployment and Work Stress

Globalisation and unemployment are two experiences which are among the most widely contested subjects in the economic debate today. Persistently, globalisation is regarded as being responsible for the increase in unemployment, mainly in unskilled labour (Wagner, 2002). Rising unemployment among educated young people is worked out as a key feature of neoliberal economic change (Jeffrey, 2008). Specifically the indirect mechanism portrayed in the literature that link globalisation and welfare state retrenchment is that globalisation induces unemployment (Huber and Stephens, 1998; 2001), because global trade policies, for example agreements in the WTO, restrict governments rights to set labour market, and public safety standards by restricting rules (Brown, 2005) that may be 'trade barriers.' Such effects of labour market adjustments to globalisation have been characterised by a rise in less secure jobs and casualisation (contract-work), 'too much work', 'not enough work' and 'no work,' and in developing countries particularly a massive shift to informal sector employment (Loewenson, 2001; ILO, 2002; WHO, 2006; Jenkins, Lee and Rodgers, 2007).

However, this shift towards employment in the informal sector in developing countries is associated with greater occupational risks and job insecurity due to lack of regulation, absence of union protection and forced occupational mobility (ILO, 2002; Kortum and Ertel, 2003). For example according to China's first *School to Work Transition Survey*, nearly 70 percent young people work in private enterprises, more than 60 percent have not signed employment contracts or only signed contracts for less than one year. Owing to the lack of regulation and union protection these young people directly become the victims of the pressure from global competition, as private sector makes every effort to increase the average working hours, lower labour costs, reduce social security and welfare to which they are entitled, and particularly most of them have never received any form of training (Libin, 2006).

In the early years of reform in China the employment rate for youth aged 16-25 years was more than 80 percent. In 1990, percentages were similar. However, according to *China Health and Nutritional Survey*, the employment rates for the same age category dropped to about 70.5 percent in 1997. On the whole the employment in the state—owned enterprises (SOEs) in China declined from 110 million in 1995 to 66 million in 2002. More dramatically manufacturing jobs decreased 15 percent between 1995—2002, i.e. from 98 million to 83 million (State Statistics, Bureau of China, 2005). During the same period, manufacturing jobs decreased by 22 million globally. Thus, China's job loss of 15 million contributed to two-thirds of the global shrinkage. The primary reasons largely attributed to this phenomenon are: privatisation of SOEs led to massive layoffs, and foreign and domestic owned private enterprises have not made up for the huge shortfall.

On the other hand studies of career mobility and income determination trends in China suggest that human capital, as a marker of abilities, is becoming increasingly important for the new aspects of the occupational attainment process (e.g., Bian, 2002; Maurer-Fazio, 2003; De-Brauw and Rozelle, 2003). Hence, in response to global economic change, the reward structures of many labour markets are changing to favor mostly those, who possess professional and technical education or experiences, considered productive. Possibly, it may be why some literature indicates that changes in youth and young adult employment in the 1990s in China are the mirror image of changes in education (Lloyd, *et al.*, 2006). This education based economic exclusion in China is accompanied by another trend i.e. private enterprises only employ young people aged between 18 and 25, and replace them with new recruiters once they are beyond that 'golden' section of age, causing severe wastage of young human resources. Indeed many public institutions have implemented the policy of 'zero staff increase', which further reduces new openings and results into fiercer employment competition (Libin, 2006).

All together, these post-reform circumstances have produced largely a new phenomenon in China called 'floating population' or unregistered temporary internal migration. This floating population is mostly young with over 80 percent less than 35 years of age (Wu & Zhou, 1996, Goodkind and West, 2002). Floaters usually get engaged in low-level construction and manufacturing jobs, household services or work in township and village enterprises or unskilled urban jobs. Studies indicate that these young migrant workers in China are much prone to stress due to the transitional nature of life, lower social status, social stigma, negative attitudes towards them (Ingrid and Russell, 2008) and financial pressure of supporting oneself and one's family back home. Additionally long working hours and fatigue could be the major factors that push these migrant workers psychologically off the edge. For example Shen, Lu, Hu, Deng, Gao and Huang, *et al.,* (1998) examined the mental health symptoms among 371 migrant workers in Shenzhen China and found that migrant workers had poorer mental health status than their non-migrant counterparts and general population in China. Particularly the psychosocial factors found to be predictive of mental health symptoms included neuroticism, psychological pressure, income, home sickness, marital problems, extroversion and introversion, living conditions, and social status. Similarly Wong, *et al.,* (2008) in their study in Shanghai China found about 16 percent mental illness among migrant workers. Committing or attempting suicide cases among migrant workers have been also reported in China (Hong and Li, 2007). Between January and May 2010, 13 young workers committed suicide at the two Foxconn production facilities in Southern China. Pressure of being away from home, and with little care and fairness from society were among the major factors behind these suicides. Chan and Pun (2010) argue that these acts can be interpreted as protest against a global labour regime characterised by labour exploitation that is widely practiced in China. Given this enormous socio-economic plight, it is not surprising to find the need for job stability, a high income and professional development as the top most considerations among young people in China (Ingrid and Russell, 2006). Research indicates that, even when unfounded, the perception of job security is sufficient to negatively affect mental health (McDonough, 2000).

Equally, in India the post-reform period has been characterised by the stagnation of employment generation in both rural and urban areas across the states. For the most part unemployment remained substantially higher for youth than across the entire working age population, and increased across all categories of young people—men or women, rural or urban (Chandrasekhar, Ghosh, and Roychowdhury, 2006). Generally speaking unemployment for youth aged

15-24 increased from 8.26 in 1994 to 10.52 percent in 2004 (ILO, 2006). The 61st round of the National Sample Survey (NSS) on employment and unemployment situation in India conducted between 2004—05 also delineates the increasing unemployment among youth. However, according to a sub-national study conducted by International Institute for Population Sciences (IIPS) and Population Council (2010: 73) between 62-76 percent of young men and between 39-60 percent of young women reported that they had ever worked. Similarly Bhaduri (2008) reveals that at the beginning of the year 2005 in India, around 56 million youth were unemployed on a particular day while 36 million remained usually unemployed.

Owing to this large pool of the unemployed around the country, many skilled workers have begun to occupy jobs for which they are over-qualified. The clashes in India on the issue of railway recruitment are obvious example showing the acuteness of the problem. Railway officials in the state of Assam received about 7.4 million applications for 2000 vacancies. Though the qualification required for these posts were Class VIII, yet graduates and postgraduates, including 20,000 engineers and 3,000 MBA degree holders applied for same jobs (EFI-Solar Foundation, 2006). These figures support the NSS (2006) observation that unemployment rate is higher among those young people (15-29 years), whose education level is higher. Unemployment rate is 9.7 percent at secondary level, 12.7 at senior secondary, 18.8 at diploma or certificate, 19.7 at graduate and 18.6 at post-graduate (The

Times of India, 2009: 2). This rising educated unemployment has become a key feature of the lives of young people in post—reform India (Jeffrey, 2008: 739), and is directly associated with the feeling of frustration and inability to move on in life. For example Sing, Sing and Rani (1996) in their study of 400 young people found that technically educated and non-technically educated unemployed youth had considerably less positive level of private and social self-concepts in them, had experienced higher social conflict and rated themselves relatively low on nearly all the attributes measuring private and social self-concepts as compared to the employed ones. Following quote from Jeffrey (2008) gives a more solid sense:

> Of course there is hope. The world runs on hope. But what can we do when 42,000 people apply for a single government post? The Indian government has given us the encouragement to become educated, but they have done nothing to encourage the creation of jobs. We are losing the will to live (p. 739).

Even those who have exploited opportunities in the globalised economy may also find mental health costs. For example anecdotal evidences suggest that the explosion in call-centre employment in India has increased presentations of substance abuse, domestic problems, depression and anxiety to local psychiatrists (Basu, 2004). This process may also unduly affect the young, who aspire to but have not attained similar employment, may be feeling left behind.

DeSouza *et al.,* (2009: 100-1) specify that unemployment is major zone of anxiety among Indian youth, and unemployed and student youth tend to report very high anxiety compared to other groups. Possibly it is because of this plight that according to IIPS and PC survey (2010) over 10 percent of young people in India reported losing sleep due to worry, 11-17 percent feeling constantly under strain, 11-15 percent feeling unhappy and depressed, and over 10 percent of young people reported feeling that they were not playing a useful role.

On the whole literature points to the fact that work-related issues manifest itself in the form of early mortality, diseases and malnutrition, prostitution, displacement and forced migration, the violence of social breakdown, fractional war, acute risk and uncertainty, vulnerability as well as a loss of existential material security. Since work has long been regarded as an important facet to mental health and the developing identity (Erikson, 1982), of this entire social plight, mental illness is associated with the highest rates (up to 90 percent) of unemployment (Harnois and Gabriel, 2000) leading individuals into economic poverty and depriving them of social networks and status within a community. Because, this is particularly true at a time when cultures and indeed, the nature of self and society (e.g. Sampson, 1989; Gergen, 1991) are changing rapidly, studies indicate that 90 percent of people affected by a severe mental illness in low and middle income countries (LMICs) are unemployed (Harnois and Gabriel, 2000). Similarly according to a cross—sectional survey in 27 countries of 732 people with diagnosed schizophrenia, 70 percent of whom were unemployed and 44 percent experienced discrimination in finding or keeping work (Thornicroft, *et al.,* 2009: 408-15). Cross-sectional and longitudinal studies however, demonstrated that specifically 'work stress' is associated with a significantly higher incidence of depression, chronic fatigue, aggression, unhealthy lifestyle habits, early retirement, burnout, alcohol abuse, summarisation and musculoskeletal disorders (Tennant 2001; Froneberg, 2003).

Conclusions

Globalisation has significant consequences for mental health. Although empirical evidence that directly links globalisation and mental health of young people in India and China is lacking. Nonetheless, such limitations are not particular to this study only. As Herman and Jane-Lopis (2005: 43) demonstrate: 'Evidence for direct causal pathways is generally strongest for the most immediate influences.' Yet the potential disadvantages of globalisation for young people in terms of mental health are clear. Since young people stand at the centre of this panorama of change characterised by cultural multiplicity and uncertainty, they may be more susceptible to stress. Socio-cultural and in particular economic transformations, which display in the transformation of labour markets, the rise of the informal sector and increasing inequalities, have a stressing influence particularly for youth.

In the context of India and China there is strong confirmation that globalisation has increased [relative] poverty and deprivation, income inequality, migration, occupational stress, educational competition and educated unemployment. Simultaneously there is evidence, which shows these variables causally linked with mental health of youth. Specifically, the major psychosocial stressors that emerged out of the post-reform circumstances in India and China, and are found correlated with mental disorders among young people are 'educated unemployment' and 'floating population.' These largely new phenomena accompanied by increased income inequality, severe educational competition and consequently higher rates of suicidal cases among lower class and student youth, substantiates the proposition that globalisation has significant consequences for mental health of young people. However, this impact of globalisation on the mental health of young people is contested and we are unable to control for the impact of other socio-cultural factors. Nevertheless, mental health disorders among youth are seldom included in the range of problems linked to globalisation.

Policy Implications

Since globalisation and its allied risk factors do not operate in a vacuum. Bridging the medical information gap, particularly the paucity of coverage of research on globalisation and mental health of youth, would help in developing preventative policies and promoting mental health of young people. However, any interventions should be supported by an integrated comprehension of globalisation as a disparate array of entangled social, economic and cultural processes. On the basis of present review, we suggest some measures which are debate oriented and need significant consideration:

In the next few decades, Asia would be one of the major sources of the growth of world's young population. Therefore, the international community with UN as the major part should make in-depth research of Asian youth problems by topic and by country in order to provide reference for the formulation of pertinent policies and measures. Furthermore, there should be a detailed and thoughtful analysis of the policies and programmes of the key global and international health institutions such as the UN, the WHO and the World Bank. For example to what extent do they promote a holistic and culturally appropriate model of mental health care?

Improving psychological and emotional well-being should be made a primary aim of public policy not just within the health sector, but also in the education, housing, employment, trade and justice sectors. Specifically, provisions for mental health of young people should be included within the framework of the Millennium Development Goals (MDGs).

Diagnostic precision and recognition of youth suicide risk must be enhanced taking into account the culture-specific context. However, psychosocial stressors, independent of psychiatric diagnosis, must also be considered as proximal determinants of suicide.

Health professionals need to be in a position to advice governments about the psychological effects of economic change and remind them of the universal human rights with respect to mental illness. For example protection of workers' rights must be improved through enhancing the legal system and expansion of the core standards of labour to cover basic conditions of employment and equitable wage.

Limitations of privatisation of education, health and other basic services must be recognized and dedicated social inclusion departments should be evolved to plan youth education, training, employment services, employment and social security as a whole.

Lastly but not least, mental health literacy is an essential life skill that must be taught before the need arises. In this regard, schools have an important role, and need to include mental health literacy as part of curriculum.

On the whole it is therefore argued that a programme for ongoing research and re-evaluation of educational, labour market and mental health policies in view of globalisation is needed in order to fully understand the complexities and patterns of youth problems. So that pertinent social policies could be framed to resolve the scandals of educated unemployment, migration, poverty and suicide etc. Fair globalisation needs integrated policies and integrated solutions.

6

Post-Soviet Transition and Young Central Asian

Majority of the today's youth cohort in Central Asian republics are born between 1985—95, a time with many monumental changes including the collapse of the Soviet Union and the transition from a Centrally controlled state to the beginning of stages of a market economy, and open political systems. In the course of these transformations, government institutions and political arenas altered dramatically. Whilst this transition opened up a range of potential opportunities, it also led to a series of specific disadvantage for young people. Where once the socialist 'cradle-to-grave' system of guaranteed jobs and education was commonplace, the emerging political economies now offer few guaranteed social entitlements. Specifically following the collapse of socialists system, majority of the state and party sponsored youth programmes throughout the region also dissolved. In what follows, we will be seeking to examine and explore this dilemma, which confronts the majority of young people in contemporary Central Asia, particularly in Uzbekistan. Drawing from the secondary sources, considering evidence on youth transitions and their vulnerability in Central Asia, we have also drawn from the studies of youth, conducted by authors, in 2012. By and large our analysis is around youth transitions in Central Asia with a major focus on the educational access and employment opportunities.

Locating Youth Transitions

Research on young people, their problems and culture etc., is much harder to date exactly. Although individual (historical, literary or ethnological) studies on young people were conducted early on, it was understood around 1990s that along with cultural emphasis, economic and health conditions of youth are also important to investigate. This emphasis undoubtedly contributed to the accumulation of a vast body of information on various aspects of living conditions, peer-group affiliations, work and leisure, social personality, tastes and selected attitudes and aspirations of young people etc. However, under the declaration of Third United Nations Development Decade, it was recommended to all countries to give priority to the mobilization and integration of youth in development, which in turn sharpened the designation of 1985 as International Youth Year. Hence the concept of youth became much a part of international discourse (UN, 1986: 12).

One of the consequences of these developments and consequent upon the contemporary socio-cultural transformations, it became a commonplace among social scientists to associate 'youth' with change (Lagree, 2004) as if young people were, per se, the carriers of innovation, as if it was not the context in which they live that shapes each new generation in its similarities or in its differences. In this respect Brown, Larson and Saraswathi (2002) is not the least interesting book emphasizing that, so far, the sociology of youth has been based upon Europe and the United States and has disseminated the images of youth from there. In reality there are markedly different 'adolescences' and 'youth' in other parts of the world that stand apart from western accounts of what does or what should happen during this transitional period between childhood and adulthood. In this area of concern the youth of former Soviet Union societies cannot be lost sight of. However, surveying the literature, it seems that we yet know less about being young and about the attitudes, aspirations and anxieties of young people in this region.

Youth studies are very young indeed, but the value of the answers to a preliminary set of questions about being young in Central Asia seems very great from an operational as well as an academic standpoint. As the World Bank (2007b) report reveals that with the Soviet Union disintegrated, many Central Asian young people saw their world turned upside down, finding their status reduced and their financial and political future uncertain. Majority of young people turned dispossessed of their right to education, work and culture. While a tiny elite youth immersed in conspicuous consumption, have monopolized places in universities and decent jobs, the dispossessed majority are struck by despair and poverty (Rigi, 2003). To borrow from Kuehnast (2002:186-98) certainly, the younger generation that is coming of age in Central Asia today is a group that finds itself worlds apart from its Soviet-raised parents, and it bears the stamp of this unique and difficult transition. In less than a decade, these countries have politically, economically, and socially reconstituted themselves. Although remnants of Soviet-era values remain entrenched among their parents' generation, the younger cohort is caught, in many ways, between two worlds. These young people know little about the once-highly centralized and socialized economy, and they have even less comprehension of how their newly decentralized governments and often corrupted new economies can offer any sort of future security for them. Yet they do recognize their own vulnerability and the vulnerability of their young Central Asian states.

Youth at the Crossroads of Transition

Young Central Asian who were seen in the Soviet system as undifferentiated and unthinking mass that required close supervision to ensure ideological loyalty, are now barely thought of by policy makers. Today young people in this region have higher rates of unemployment. Speaking generally, almost one out of every three i.e. 33 percent people aged 15-29 years are unemployed in Central Asia (US Census Bureau, 2005).[7] Surveys of young people in Eastern Europe, and Central Asia, carried out for the World Bank, 2007 *World Development Report,* indicate that access to jobs, along with physical security, are young peoples' greatest concerns, because this region witnessed a year-over-year increase in unemployment, which stands at 9.7 percent, up from 9.5 per cent in 2004 (ILO, 2006). Consequently about 4.1 million young people in Central Asia are living on less than one Dollar a day (UN, 2005). Before going to discuss the scenario of unemployment and poverty among Central Asian youth, let's have a brief discussion on their access to education and its allied issue in Central Asia.

Educational Access

As elsewhere in the world young people in Central Asian republics are pursuing education partly due to 'push' factors such as the lack of jobs especially for teenage labour market entrants, and partly due to 'pull' factors like the hope that attaining further qualifications would enhance labour market returns. But this is not a common feature taking into account country contexts. In some countries, for example Turkmenistan and Uzbekistan, there is a strict control over the admission processes and the number of students admitted to higher education is limited. Hence when elsewhere

---

[7] Figures are from United States Census Bureau. 2005. Available at: http://www.census.gov/ipc/www /idbsum.html [last accessed, 25 March 2011].

the systems have expanded in response to demands, these countries are taking a refuge. In fact in order to boost their own budgets, public universities in these countries have increased fee charges. Private universities have further revamped this issue.

Figure 6.1: Young People Paying for Education (in %) at State-run Establishments in Some Selected CIS Countries (as of 2004-05 Academic Year).

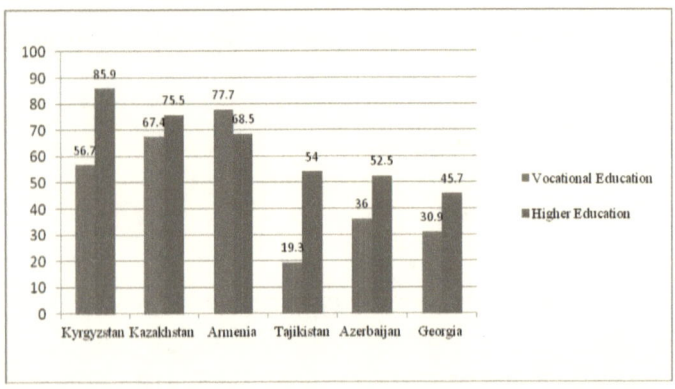

Source: CIS Inter-State Statistical Committee, 2004 and Baskakova, 2007.

Though in few countries of the region the number of entrants has gone up with the introduction of private educational institutions like Kyrgyzstan, where there were just nine institutions of higher education in 1991, which increased to 51 by 2006 including more than 20 private universities. During this period the number of students rose from just over 58,000 to over 200,000 (Roberts, 2010: 541).

But it doesn't mean the absence of dilemma for an "ordinary" Central Asian youth. Corruption in educational institutions in Central Asia, which is more reported and debated (Trilling 2009) has put the potential of many youth at risk. Well-off students often pay for entrance and grades and consequently gain high paid jobs. The students who somehow manage to pay for vocational and higher education report concerns about the quality and relevance of education in preparing them for the labour market. Such phenomenon has significantly led to scepticism on the part of administrators and the public about the significance and quality of higher education. Yet, currently for many young Central Asian, "being a student" is a more pleasing status than being unemployed or under-employed in menial occupations (see DeYoung et al., 2006). For example by 2006 in Almaty, less than 40 percent of higher education graduates were obtaining jobs. The rest were believed to be unemployed or working casually as drivers, in consumer services etc. (Zhakenovnd, 2006).

Unemployment and Poverty

Consequent upon the collapse of Soviet Union, almost all Central Asian countries experienced similar period of sharp and steep economic dwindling up to the beginning of twenty first century. Since then, these countries have officially recovered, but at different rates. Nevertheless, there has been a kind of predisposition all over the region that benefits of growth flow mainly to advantaged sections of population, who have either retained old or with their new tactics and networks found new full-time regular employment (Roberts, 2009). Since, youth are at the forefront of every economic niche, the flow of advantages to advantaged, has created a huge socio-economic cleavage among youth in Central Asia. While the advantaged youth are immersed in conspicuous consumption, have occupied places in universities and good jobs, the "ordinary" youth live in dire poverty. The economic niche available to them consists of menial jobs in the informal sector (Regi, 2003).

Thus while Communism spread 'modern' forms of employment into all regions and to all young people, who among other things were proffered with 'modern' public services—health, education, policing and public administration. The current low labour productivity and inefficient employment practices have however, deteriorated their social and cultural growth. In some of the Central Asian republics like Tajikistan, Turkmenistan, Kyrgyzstan and to some extent in Uzbekistan these problems are rife and most of the young people have become even poorer, which has resulted into the re-ruralization (Roberts, 2010: 540). Consequently the magnitude of the young workforce engaged in agriculture has risen. For instance, in 1991 in Kyrgyzstan, agriculture employed 27 percent of the workforce; by 2000, the figure had risen to over 50 percent (Kuznetsova 2003). Working on plots of land, seeking and taking on casual jobs are among other things that most of the Central Asia youth are engaged with. Hence under-employment has also become widespread in these countries.

Of the more recent, there are some differences like young people in Kyrgyzstan, Tajikistan and Uzbekistan strive to move outside their countries to obtain jobs especially in Kazakhstan or in the Caspian oil fields and if they are failing their next choice is Moscow (Thieme, 2007). Nevertheless, this is again not a common feature and can be misleading. Direct employment in the oil and gas industries accounts for only a small proportions of these countries workforce and unemployment, under-employment and poverty remains a serious problem, even in the Kazakhstan and to some extent in Russia as well (Kazakhstan News Bulletin, 2005).

For many young people the rational response to this plight of unemployment, underemployment and poverty is indeed to leave, a phenomenon, which has become a key policy issue in several Central Asian Republics. But there are other domains as well such as the ethno-cultural and ethno-political discomfort which has not been focused over to be a cause of post-Soviet Central Asian migratory flows. The new ethnic minorities, which emerged upon the break-up of the Soviet Union, comprised the majority of migratory flows of all age groups. However, locating the cause at ground level reveals that this story has bulk of its content related to youth issues. Some ethnic minorities returned to what they consider to be 'home', but majority felt uncomfortable with the changes induced by independence (Agadjanian, *et al.*, 2008), especially when required to learn a new official language.

Minority Youth Confronts Language Politics

In the nation building project of almost each Central Asian republic, language as elsewhere, constituted an important element. But the issues that emerged thereon proffer a special case study that I shall be discussing in next chapter. Herein I shall be offering a brief account of the issues allied with the representation and treatment of minority youth in educational institutions in the Central Asian Republics.

Language is a politico-culturally a sensitive concern in Central Asia and to articulate something about this, it is very much important to keep in consideration that the Central Asian States were themselves created by Soviet power. None of them existed as distinct nation until the 1920s. Equally Soviet powers organized the ethno-cultural distinctiveness of these nations that were finally allied with the emergence of today's Central Asia republics as well as the nationalising of languages specific to these States and their populations. In fact, "this was a natural product of the Soviet approach to nationality issues which linked territory, population and language" (Fierman 2009: 1207). Even if, a major language in each republic was the titular language of the now-gone Soviet entities, the Soviet command nevertheless, in some or other ways encouraged the non-titular languages. Specifically, Russian was encouraged (but never given an official State language status) to foster the configuration for a blended Soviet identity and culture. Indeed, Russian happened to be a "career language", especially for pursuing education and jobs.

Nonetheless, since the collapse of Soviet system, the overall shift in language as a symbol of nation-building and power throughout Central Asia has been altogether, away from Russian, representing a revival of specific 'nationality' and thereby a promotion of titular languages encourage by the political and cultural elites of these now-gone Soviet republics. Such undertaking however, has not been smooth sailing especially in the case of minority representations throughout post-Soviet Central Asia. Political elites of these republics, seeking to cultivate a ground for national-building, have decided on multiple language policies. For instance, Uzbekistan's president has opted 'nationalisation', eulogizing Uzbeks above other ethnic groups in the country. On the other hand, Niyazov, the president of Turkmenistan opted for a bold policy of Turkmenisation and de-Russification.

Thus since the independence of these Central Asian States, major drive of laws and decrees concerning language has been to revive titular languages both in public and private domains and downplay the Russian language. This has been altogether most strictly pursued in Turkmenistan and Uzbekistan, wherein nearly all non-Turkmen and non-Uzbek schools were either turned into mixed schools or totally closed, thereby reducing *lingual* space for minorities. Specifically Russian language was removed as an obligatory subject in the school curriculum. To a certain degree, Kazakhstan as well promoted the status of its titular language. Albeit, legislation in Kazakhstan, opted for a shift of all official work to be administered in the state language, but all that has not been successful to the expected levels. Indeed, language law passed in 1997 downplayed Russian from being a 'language of cross-national communication,' rather introduced an equally vague status for it as the language 'used officially on a par with Kazakh in state organisations and organs of local self-government' (Fierman 1998: 179).

To somewhat similarly the extent of language politics in Kyrgyzstan and Uzbekistan has been also in a dilemmatic condition, but not as problematic as has been the case in Turkmenistan, though the role of Russian in Uzbekistan has increasingly dwindled, since its independence in 1991. Kyrgyzstan due to certain factors pursued change in language status in ways similar to Kazakhstan. Russian has been given an 'official' status, but not raised to a status of state language, while Uzbek continued to used in all levels of education specifically in the country's South.

Still in this context and given the laws and decrees passed and adopted, Uzbekistan offers perhaps the best instance of the intricacy in deciding a language regulation. Since, 1991, Uzbek government conceded a number of legislations related to language, particularly in order to develop an independent Uzbek national culture. In 1989, Uzbek was made the official state language and Russian the official 'language of inter-ethnic communication' (Smith et al. 1998). Moreover, government officials were obligated to be able to carry out their jobs in Uzbek. Perhaps, the primary motive of this law was to elevate the status of ethnic Uzbeks, over and above other nationalities in Uzbekistan. Yet another law was passed in 1993 to convert the alphabet from Cyrillic script to Latin, signifying a de-Russification and a new internationalisation (Landau and Kellner-Heinkele 2001). In 1995, Uzbekistan amended the state language law, wherein Russian was stripped from having a special status.

For young people, the repercussion of these language reforms in Uzbekistan is directly related to a school to work transition. Indeed complicated the situation is of the newer generation of youth, who have been formally pursuing education in Uzbek and for whom Russian is a non-native language. As of 2004 in Uzbekistan, there were only 93 schools that taught entirely in Russian. Andijan, the third-largest city in the country, has only one Russophone school. More than 600 schools offer bilingual Russian-Uzbek instruction, or trilingual education in Russian, Uzbek, and Karakalpak, but this number was twice as large in 1992 (Peyrouse, 2008:18-19).

This process has many repercussions, but the major one is directly related to motivations for departure, which are indeed multiple in Central Asia, and pose at the same time economic, social, and political concerns, but the linguistic nationalization carried out in each republic provides a strong impetus for minority youth to emigrate. Absence of official support, the strong feelings that especially Russian minority youth hold toward Central Asian languages, which they perceive as useless give impetus to the principal cause of emigration i.e. absence of a future, or the perception of such. Among the minority nationalities of Central Asia, Russians however, dominate in terms of candidates for emigration, though one can note a similar based desire to leave in other groups such as the Germans, Ukrainians, Belarusians, and Tatars. In recent past, the ethno-cultural and political forces of migration have dwindled in some Central Asian republics like Kazakhstan and Kyrgyzstan, the phenomenon has turned to be even more complex in republics such as Uzbekistan given its rigid nationalistic narrative and political realities.

The Scenario of Uzbek Youth

Uzbekistan, the most populous country of Central Asian republics, having 27.7 million people in which 64 percent i.e. 17 million are under the age of thirty (CIA, *World Fact Book,* 2009). Constitutionally Uzbekistan provides for democracy and asserts that highest value shall be the freedom, honor, dignity and other inalienable rights of human being. However, many international bodies such as World Bank, IMF, ICG, Human Rights Watch, Amnesty International as well as US Department of State and Council of European Union, define Uzbekistan as an authoritarian State with limited civil rights and characterize its politics not by liberalization, but rather by sustained, if not, increasing authoritarianism.

This definition possess a lot of strength because despite more than two decades of independence, Uzbekistan continues to rely on economic philosophy that stresses social stability over market reforms and effectively retains many elements of Central Planning and the States key role as did its Soviet predecessor. But the success of these strategies is not guaranteed in the present day world, because, being rhetorically committed to a programme of political liberalization and economic reforms, may be why Uzbekistan continues to suffer serious economic challenges, unemployment is rising and living standards are declining. While official unemployment is very low, i.e. 3 percent according to the Uzbek Ministry of Labour as of 2007, underemployment especially in rural areas is estimated to be at least 20 percent (CIA, Uzbekistan, 2009). Particularly among young people aged between 15-24 years, the World Bank in 2006 estimated unemployment at 13 percent (World Bank, 2007a).

Figure 6.2: Percentage of Uzbek Youth Employment by Sector

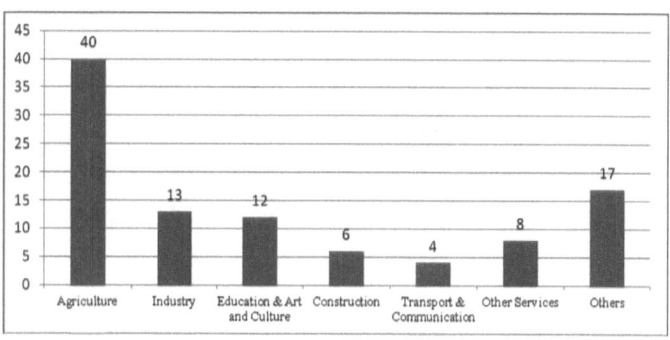

Source: Uzbek Economic Trends, Third Quarter 2004, NIS/TACIS Services, Tashkent.

In the sphere of education, the enrolment in primary schools of Uzbekistan dropped to 88 percent and in higher education dropped from 14 percent in 1991 to about 6.4 percent in 2001(World Bank, 2003: 93). Although, there seem to be some reversal in past two three years, the compulsory and forced recruitment of children between grades five to nine (age 10-15 years) on cotton fields is still there. It is worth-noting here that for male population, they have to by law serve for one year in the military (Ziyaeva, 2006: 5-7), which now seems to be the part of the present governments strategy for political survival. Because the growing regional unrest like *Ferghana, Ququon* and *Karshi* uprising in November 2004, and May 2005 *Andijan* uprising are indicators of the current regimes inability to ensure regional elite loyalty through traditional patronage networks. Motivated by this policy failure, present leadership now seeks to mobilize youth as an alternative base for political support.

At the centre of this youth politics are two institutions: the *Kamolot* Youth Organization and the Tashkent Islamic University. President Karimov's numerous books have been made part of the higher education curriculum and must be mastered to enter university and pass graduation examinations (Glinchy, 2006: 3-12). Students are taught to conform to the official lines and critical thinking is often met with particular suspicion. Precisely youth and their culture are extensively supervised, with young people having almost no scope for discussion and debate their own country's political and administrative setup. A fear factor is highly prevalent among Uzbek youth.

To certain degree this politicizing of youth and their culture works to limit the centrifugal pull of regional and familial identities, nonetheless, in a long run it would undermines not only the prospects for political pluralism and employability. Rather this stultifying control also produces a generation, fearful of open discussion and seldom able to form independent opinions, and is intimately linked to the other major concerns in young people's lives.

Final Thoughts

In World Development Report 2007, these republics have been described as receiving 'demographic dividend.' Empirically the concept of 'demographic dividend' refers to the rise in the rate of economic growth due to increase in the share of working-age people in a population. For instance in Uzbekistan as of 2009, 64 percent population belongs to under thirty year's age. However, the prime concern here is that if this young population is not absorbed by economy, the promise of the 'dividend' would turn out to be a burden and problematic too. Studies suggest that a so-called youth bulge—a high proportion of youth in comparison to the total population represents a serious potential source of conflict and if left with no alternative but unemployment and poverty, are likely to join underground and illegal movements to seek alternative choices outside conventional society and find crime and drugs an escape from their often unattractive everyday life.

The statistics of socio-health status of youth in Central Asia already show such instances of problematic. According to the UN Aids Report, 2008; since 2001, HIV prevalence in Central Asia has risen by 66 percent bringing the number of people living with HIV to 1.5 million in 2008 and making it the only region where HIV prevalence clearly remains on the rise. The epidemic here is concentrated more among people who inject drugs and sex workers (half million injecting drug users & 80 percent of sex workers in Central Asia & CIS respectively are under the age of 25 years) (World Bank 2007b). There is more than half million injecting drug users under the age of 25 years in Central Asia, of whom above 80 percent are likely to become HIV aids infected (UN, 2008 *Aids Update*). In Tajikistan, Kazakhstan and Kyrgyzstan the number of people aged 15-24 years living with HIV almost quadrupled between 2003 and 2005 and doubled in Azerbaijan and Georgia (UN, 2005). However, In Uzbekistan the most recent data is for the year 2008, which shows HIV cases tripled between 2003 and 2007. Flesh trade, which has been boosted by extreme poverty and social breakdown, is also found at the nexus of drugs and crime. For example The 2009 *Trafficking in Person Report* shows Uzbekistan as a source country of women and girls trafficked to USA, UAE, Japan, Israel and India etc (US Deptt. of State, 2009).[8]

---

[8] US Department of State. *Trafficking in Person Report, 2009*. USDS, 2009. Available at: http:// www.state. gov/documents / organization/123357.pdf

That said, if demography is destiny, then the destiny of Central Asia is appalling and in a long run may pose many dangers. Hence, there should be a serious consideration on the part of academicians, policy makers, public intellectuals and administrators at the issues of school to work transitions in Central Asian republics and a support for holistic and integrated developmental process must be put forward.

7

Language Politics and Minority Youth in Central Asia

After independence, Central Asian regimes sought to assume much of the authority over their affairs which had heretofore been exercised by Moscow, and which they could hardly have anticipated that in late summer 1991 they would acquire full independence. However, their independence came under very unfavourable economic conditions. Despite their vast mineral wealth and consequent potential for economic growth, this region inherited an overspecialized economy e.g. cotton economy in Uzbekistan, a major ecological disaster, and a low standard of living, had a very high birth rate and an overabundant and poorly trained labour force (Fierman, 1995).

In this backdrop Central Asian regimes emphasised upon short-term political stability. By and large this emphasis made these regimes much less willing to initiate economic reforms, open to and suitable for global economy. Instead a heavy accentuation has been on state-building and the creation of symbols that could unite people under political tutelage (Light, 2011). Indeed such an 'inventing of tradition' is still important as strategy of political survival in these regimes, particularly in Uzbekistan, Turkmenistan and Tajikistan, wherein we contend that the concept of culture has become discursively useful in these nation-state polities in which what Mann (1995) argues that bureaucracy and military capacities are developed to manage a territory as a cohesive unit: language, religion, and shared ideologies are some of the technologies of rule for managing territorial states.

Such a type of nationalism in Central Asia surfaces from a protracted tradition of fabricating politically meaningful identities that at the moment can be exercised to bond the state more powerfully to citizen's lives. By means of the work of people in different bureaucratic and public contexts, the state expands a congeries of symbolic exchange relationships with citizens. This soft, participatory rule acquires strength through the material realities of policing, resource control, state borders, schooling and bureaucratic interactions (Light, 2011). In this context however, linguistic diversity still constitutes a particularly prominent policy-challenge for these Central Asian polities. Since, traditional notions of State have often believed the existence of linguistically homogenized demos as illustrated in the classical model of the nation-state (Koenig, 2001: 55). Nonetheless, the increasing recognition of linguistic human rights in international law has contributed, in conjunction with other social and economic dynamics, to a sweeping transformation of the model of the nation-state, offering new normative standards for democratic modes of governing multi-lingual societies. These include, not least, the recognition of the human rights of linguistic minorities (Ibid. p.55).

Language Politics in Central Asia

As elsewhere in the world, the language has been one of the key factors causative to the cultural diversity of Central Asian regimes (Smith, et al. 1998). However, political shifts and economic factors have exerted considerable influence over language policies in Central Asia. Because language issues have played a major part in the nationalist discourse and in the shaping of new and transformed national identities in the post-Soviet states, they have become highly politicised as languages were/are involved in *defining the new state*. Right after independence, these new governments were faced with a political dilemma of identification. On the one hand, they were newly independent states trying to assert themselves as nations with Uzbek, Kyrgyz or Kazak as their sole national language. On the other, the strong monolingual ideology was needed to build a new nation/state, to reverse decades of language shift and to unite ethnic groups, who were divided (Coleman, et al. 2005).

Given that, nationalist leaders in these regimes strived for national identity in both the political and cultural domains, which led many scholars and researchers to present these countries as awakening culturally after a long Soviet slumber (Adams, 1999). Uzbekistan in particular offers an interesting case study of this stance, where as elsewhere in Central Asia, the basic objective of language policies contend with Russian-speaking intelligentsias, numerous ethnic minorities, and sizeable Russian communities backed by the Russian Federation—all presenting major challenges to facing the legacy of Soviet rule (Kellner-Heinkele and Landau, 2011).

Thus close to Soviet language policy—which was highly centralized, designed and controlled by Moscow, and which was characterized first and foremost by the dominance and influence of the Russian language, present-day Central Asian language policies are centralized rather than decentralized, wherein the basic motive is de-Russification and revival of local long-established lineal and genealogical links as evidenced by rewriting of history books, propagating new national myths, changing the alphabet to Latin, replacing Soviet place names with local ones and changing the status of languages (Radnitz, 2006). Therefore, of the several factors, which continue to influence language policies throughout Central Asia, the most central according to Fierman (1995), is the status of the [titular] language during the late Soviet era, wherein de-Russification is expressed in promoting the titular language to the first place and downgrading Russian to the second.

This process however has not been without predicaments. Implicitly or explicitly, it underlies irredentism, ethnic conflict, mass migration and ethnic cleansing, and the redrawing of national and regional boundaries. Indeed some held that the key element in such politicised linguistics and the discourse of nation-building in many of the post-Soviet states is myths about language (Kellner-Heinkele, 2011).

Language policies and Language Use in Central Asia

The five state language laws passed by the Central Asian Supreme Soviets in 1989 and 1990 were first and foremost language status laws, which laid down the rights and obligations in the use of languages and the choice of language in specific public settings and official functions (Schlyter, 2001). To some extent, these laws were directed to language corpus issues for instance alphabet, vocabulary and grammar, which later were to be regulated by further laws and suggestion within the few years following the first round of enactments of state language laws and while they were simultaneously the focus of attention in public debates encouraged by the work performed on establishing state languages.

However, as Schlyter (2001) holds that 'when a nation becomes a state, bureaucracy generally makes its entrance into the organisation of that state. The Central Asian language policies, or attempts at language policies, are good examples of this. They are bureaucratic state language policies. With the inclusion of bureaucracy, dynamism and flexibility are easily lost.' Thus much of the follow-up work of language law implementation in Central Asia at the present moment is concerned with not the status but the state of languages. For instance the 'Law on State Language of the Republic of Uzbekistan' was adopted on 21 October 1989, edited in 1995 and amended in 2004. In the 1989 version, Article 1 reads as follows:

> The state language of the Republic of Uzbekistan is Uzbek. The Republic of Uzbekistan will ensure utmost development and functioning of the Uzbek language in the political, social, economic and cultural life of the Republic. The development and free use of the Russian language as the language of inter-ethnic communication of the people of the former Soviet Union in the territory of Uzbekistan will be ensured.

Though there have been some reformation in this law in 1995 and 2004, but in essence, this law is practised as per 1989 version. Equally in Kazakhstan the Language Law now defines and reaffirms the political and cultural significance of the state language. The article 4 of the Law states: 'It is the duty of every citizen of the Republic of Kazakhstan to master the state language'. The dominance of the state language was reinforced by the 1998 government decree on the use of the State Language in State institutions. This stance is pretty clear given the recent statistics from these regimes.

The Central Asian regimes make a distinction between state languages, official languages and languages of inter-ethnic communication. The scenario as of 2010 was as follows:

Table 7.1: Official Status of Different Languages in Central Asia

Country	State language	Official and inter-ethnic communication
Kazakhstan	Kazakh	Russian (official)
Kyrgyzstan	Kyrgyz	Russian (official)
Tajikistan	Tajik	Russian (inter-ethnic communication)
Turkmenistan	Turkmen	Russian and English (inter-ethnic communication)
Uzbekistan	Uzbek	Russian (inter-ethnic communication)

Source: Aminov, et al. Central Asia Regional Data Review, Vol.2 (1): 1-29. Spring, 2010

However, on observing the ground, the situation that appears here seems relatively complicated. For example according to an opinion survey conducted by the *Department for the Development of Languages of the Ministry of Culture* in 2004 in fourteen localities of Kazakhstan, the percentage of respondents who consider their native language to be Kazakh or Russian is as follows:

Table 7.2: Opinion about Native Languages in Kazakhstan

Language	2000 (%)	2004 (%)
Kazakh	51.9	52.6
Russian	37.3	38.7
Other Languages	10.8	8.7

Source: Z. Shaukenova, Director of Institute of Comparative Social Research 'CESSI-Kazakhstan', 'Yazykovaya situaziya V Kazakhstane' (Language Situation in Kazakhstan') http://www.cessi.ru/ index. php?id=169 (accessed 8 Dec. 2011).

Similarly in Uzbekistan the Russian is considered to be the native language of the majority of the non-Uzbek population, which include Tajik (4.5%), Kazakh (25%), Kara-kalpak (2%), Kyrgyz (1%) and also Turkmen, Tatars, Koreans are there.[9] According to the Russian Information Agency (RIA), in 2003, 57% of Uzbekistan's population spoke at least some Russian.

Table 7.3: Status of Different Language in the In/formal Settings in Uzbekistan

Languages	Formal Settings (%)	Informal Settings (%)
Only Uzbek	11	19
Uzbek and Russian	38	-
Only Russian	39	20
Tajik and Russian	-	21
Tajik	-	38

Source: Aminov, et al. Central Asia Regional Data Review, Vol.2 (1): 1-29. Spring, 2010

Hence, it is Russian being spoken highly in both formal and informal settings in Uzbekistan. In fact according to some sources, as much as 70 percent of the population speaks at least some Russian. A recent survey of students, teachers, professors and bureaucrats found that only one percent of respondents use English in their professional activities and read publications in English. Still on the other hand there are sources signifying that the Persian-speaking Tajik population of Uzbekistan may be as large as 25 percent to 30 percent of the total population[10],

---

9 'Ethnic Atlas of Uzbekistan', Open Society Institute, 2002, p. 452.
10 Richard Foltz. 1996. 'The Tajiks of Uzbekistan', *Central Asian Survey*, 15(2): 213-216.

however, these assessments aren't grounded on authentic reports, because Tajik is the dominant language spoken in the cities of Bukhara and Samarkand only. So how come it might constitutes 25-30 percent of the total language use in Uzbekistan.

In Turkmenistan as well discrepancies can be observed between the population as per ethnic origin and actual language use, where Primary language use and mother tongue self-identification is used as the primary language by 72 percent of the population, Russian by 12 percent, Uzbek 9 percent, and others 7 percent.[11]

Correspondingly in Kyrgyzstan, as per the official Kyrgyz statistics, for the predominant majority of population and the ethnic groups the primary language use is as given in below table:

Table 7.4: Status of Different Language in Kyrgyzstan

Ethnic groups	Percentage of total population	Percentage of language users
Kyrgyz	70.9	71.4
Uzbek	14.3	14.4
Russian	7.8	9
Dungan	1	1
Other	5.8	4.2

Source: Kyrgyz National Statistics Committee, *National Population Census 2009*, < https://www.stat.kg> (accessed 03 July 2012)

Thus, given all the evidence presented above and after having further scrutinised an outline of language use and

---

[11] CIA Factbook, Turkmenistan, (2003) https://www.cia.gov/library/publications/the-worldfactbook/ geos/tx.html (accessed 10 April 2012)

regulations pertinent to different realms of public life in Central Asian regimes viz. education, government, the judiciary, business and the economy and advertising; we were witness to a very mixed and complicated picture, wherein we could observe that minority groups are put to an exclusion.

In this respect, however, there is no big problem about the legal and political status of minorities than the medium of instruction in the school. It is at the school level that the genuine linguistic diversity is put to test. As in Kyrgyzstan for example, the major issue related to language is in the education sector, which involves the mounting pressure to use Kyrgyz, and constant government resistance to the growth of Uzbek language schools.

Educational Institutions and the Dilemmas of Minorities Groups

Language issues have become emerging major problems with representation and treatment of minorities and indigenous groups in educational institutions in the Central Asian Republics. Research shows that for minority-language children, one barrier to educational achievement is the language of schooling. Indeed in industrialized countries, where education finances are relatively strong, minority-language children still often have a higher dropout rate, lower attendance rate, poorer achievement scores, lower rates of secondary school graduation and of continuation to post-secondary study, and more frequent placement in non-academic or vocational streams compared to majority-language children (Watt and Roessingh, 2001).

Nonetheless, as said earlier, in Central Asia, the politico-cultural transition has shaped this situation in a more problematic way. In this juncture, the most hit are the Russian and European minorities, who once dominated the educational sector, because on the one hand the role of Russian language is not less than an important asset, the native language and the lingua franca for inter-ethnic and international communication of these ethnic minorities living in the region, but for many of them it is the language of business across and beyond the borders of Central Asia. On the other, however, the situation of Russian language in educational sector has quickly deteriorated in all five republics, for reasons as political as they are practical (Peyrouse, 2008). Since Russia is to Central Asia, what West is to East and South Asia, many parents (not pertaining to minorities only) deem it more important for their children have a good command of Russian than of the language they are taught at school. They realize that a good command of Russian is crucial for access to information, higher education and interesting job opportunities and the overall development and improvement. However, schools in Kyrgyzstan do not provide enough time or satisfactory methodology for children to learn to communicate in Russian.[12]

Equally in Turkmenistan, higher education in Russian has been banned. Many students including Russian-speaking ethnic Turkmens fail to pass the Turkmen language test

---

[12] Beatrice Schulter. 2003. 'Language and Identity: The Situation in Kyrgyzstan and the Role of Pedagogy.' http://www.cimera.org/files/other/en/11_Bea_en.pdf (accessed 013 October 2012)

required for access to higher education. Therefore, students from ethnic minorities are simply excluded. Given this plight most of the parents [in CAR's] often make the choice of Russian or even English-for their children, because they believe it results in better education and employment.[13] In fact, in Turkmenistan, classes in Russian disappeared from course offerings soon after independence. Whereas the country had nearly 2,000 Russian-language schools in 1991, fewer than 100 existed in 2000, and only 50 in 2005. Additional 50 or so schools teach partially in Russian and partially in Turkmen.[14]

In Tajikistan as per the reports by Niyozov (2001), proficiency for many minority students specifically of East Iranian and *Pamiri* languages are insufficient to comprehend lessons adequately, especially since the curriculum and texts are too abstract for comprehension in their second language. Weak expressive ability in Tajik makes some unable to express their understanding clearly causing them to receive lower marks and to feel reluctant to speak in class due to anxiety about being ridiculed as well as receiving poor marks.

As for Uzbekistan is concerned, it had only 93 schools that taught entirely in Russian as of 2004. Andijan, the third-largest city in the country, has only one Russophone school. More than 600 schools offer bilingual Russian-Uzbek instruction, or trilingual education in Russian, Uzbek, and

---

[13] Sultan, J. 2003. *Kyrgyz Language Barrier.* Available at: http://www.iwpr.org/pdf/I916.pdf (Accessed 19 August 2012).

[14] Kadyrov, Sh. 2003. *Natsiia plemen. Etnicheskie istoki, transformatsiia, perspektivy gosudarstvennosti v Turkmenistane.* Moscow: RAN, p. 155.

Karakalpak, but this number was twice as large in 1992 (Peyrouse, 2008:18-9). Somewhat similarly the process of *Kazakhization* of the education system has proved more complex.

Thus on the whole, it would be inferred that the cultural sphere, which for the most part include the education system is by and large limited for minorities in Central Asian republics. Nevertheless, given the huge socio-economic repercussions of this process, some nations, like Uzbekistan, that just a short time ago was enthusiastically striving to reduce Russia's cultural influence, are now experiencing a modest revival in the use of the Russian language (Weitz, 2008). Still, contemporarily this process has increased the predicaments for minorities. For minority people the rational response to this plight is to leave, a phenomenon that has become a key policy issue in several Central Asian Republics.

Response of Minorities

The motivations for departure are multiple, and pose at the same time economic, social, and political concerns, but the linguistic nationalization carried out in each republic provided a strong impetus to emigrate. Absence of official support, the strong feelings that especially Russian minorities hold toward Central Asian languages, which they perceive as useless give impetus to the principal cause of emigration i.e. absence of a future, or the perception of such, for the younger generations and the degradation of the education system.

Among the minority nationalities of Central Asia, Russians however, dominate in terms of candidates for emigration, though one can note a similar based desire to leave in other groups such as the Germans, Ukrainians, Belarusians, and Tatars. Thus republics of Central Asia hold the unfortunate record of having the highest numbers of would be Russian emigrants. According to some recent surveys, the proportion of individuals who wanted to emigrate was much higher—43 percent in Uzbekistan, 36 percent in Kyrgyzstan, 66 percent in Tajikistan—mainly to provide a future for their children. Among the specified cause the linguistic policy has been the predominant (Peyrouse, 2008). Thus a primary consequence of the changing language patterns has been emigration by Russian-speakers, many of whom are skilled labourers and professionals. The emigration trend has been heaviest in Kazakhstan, where, according to some estimates, up to 2 million Russian speakers have left the country.[15] A similar trend has been reported in Kyrgyzstan, although the overall numbers are far lower.

Concluding Remarks

As elsewhere in the world, the language has been one of the key factors causative to the cultural diversity of Central Asian regimes. However, with new socio-political contexts emerging in present-day Central Asia, most identities in this region are

---

[15] Berniker, M. 2003. Examining Linguistic Trends in Central Asia. Available online at: http://www.eurasianet.org/54109 (accessed 11 Oct. 2012).

in a sensitive state of readjustment and redefinition, be they ethnic, cultural, national or any combination of these, wherein a heavy accentuation has been on state-building and the creation of symbols that could unite people under political tutelage. Because in this context language issues have played a major part in the nationalist discourse and in the shaping of new and transformed national identities in the post-Soviet states, they have become highly politicised as languages were/are involved in *defining the new state*. Thus political shifts have exerted considerable influence over language policies in Central Asia. Such a nation-building and everyday nationalism influenced however, greatly the institutional participation of minority and indigenous groups, insofar as it affected their material well being, by creating language barriers and put their children at a disadvantage at school. By phasing out the minority languages from the official sphere, or by establishing unofficial quotas favouring the majority is the leadership sending signals to minorities that they are unwanted. Still language policies in and of themselves may not be objectionable, but may impact insofar as they hinder minority peoples opportunities for professional advancement or put their children at a disadvantage at school by creating language barriers.

8

Youth and Transnational Migration in Central Asia

Migration and dispersion of people is a natural and global phenomenon dating back to the nomadic period. Even when human beings started forming communities, they experienced temporary, seasonal, or permanent migration from their original area of settlement (Panday, 2009: 168). However, with the contemporary advancements in the means of transportation and communication, this process has become more intensified, speedy and pronounced, resulting into a key global phenomenon.

In this context, UNFPA's report on *The State of World Population* (2006) firmly accounts that today the number of people living outside their country of birth is larger than at any other time in history, and brings fore that the total population in the 'nation of immigrants' would comprise the seventh largest on earth, larger than Bangladesh, the Russian Federation, Nigeria or Japan if they all lived in the same place. According to the United Nations estimates the number of people living outside their country of origin has risen from 120 million in 1990 to about 214 million in 2011. Specifically as per UN *Human Development Report* (2010), migrants account for approximately 3.1 percent of world population.[16]

Obviously then, such a wide-scale movement of people is as much a defining feature of globalization as the movement of goods, services, and capital. In fact, accompanied by the global remittances equalled $150-200 billion (Panday, 2009:170), a level that is larger than the current size of the economy of any country in the world except the United States, this cross-national flows of capital and labour have been directly implicated in the structuring and development of the global economy throughout world history. In this respect, capital and labour movements are both a means of producing and an outcome of the global economy (Sanderson and Kentor, 2008:514-15).

Nonetheless, this contemporary global migration is not a smooth sailing experience as some classical literature makes us to believe. Instead, it is a dynamic phenomenon involving many twists and turns, not to mention the issues of integration of immigrants, brain drain, exploitation of immigrants, human trafficking, security and border controls,

---

[16] Figures are from UNDP. 2010. *Human Development Report.* Available online at: http://hdr.undp.org/ en/media/HDR_2009_EN_Complete. pdf (accessed August 2011).

labour market impacts (including low wages, job stability and unemployment), replacement migration and demographic ageing, return migration, gender perspectives in migration etc. Specifically, in the post-Communist, post-9/11 world, migration and immigration have become central area of public interest.

Since the attack on the World Trade Center and ensuing crises, such as the Madrid and London bombings, immigration fears have fused with those over national security. The collapse of the Soviet Union and wars in Bosnia and Kosovo led to a new wave of economic migrants, guest-workers and asylum seekers in Europe (Edmunds, 2006:554). In particular, amidst the political changes that swept through Central Asia following the collapse of Soviet Union in 1989, the right to migrate was synonymous in the minds of many with the establishment of democracy. A mosaic of migration patterns (ethnically based migrations, return migration, labour migration, transit migration) gathered pace during the 1990s throughout the region and was further inflated by huge numbers of refugees, asylum-seekers and displaced persons as conflict and war broke out in different areas, notably in the Caucasus and south-east Europe (Tonelli, 2003).

Against such backdrops, considering the causes and consequences of international migration, is increasingly becoming an important concern, essentially for the edifice of immigration policies. Despite the magnitude of the issue, however, the theoretical rationalization of international migration remain largely inconsistent. Studies of migration are generally located at the level of the individual, the household or the level of social structure (Sanderson and Kentor, 2008). Individual—and household-level migration studies typically consider the decision-making process behind migration. Here, are the neo-liberal economic accounts predominant, as individuals or households are recurrently argued to act rationally based upon an assessment of the costs and risks allied with movement. Conversely structural-level studies are more gripped in understanding how the social context shapes the decision to migrate independently of individual and household-level behaviour. Based on this theoretical carriage, there has been a trend in social science literature on 'mezzo-level' migration studies, which are related to the considerations of how social networks are implicated in the migration process (Portes, 1997a). Indeed, currently transnational networks have been the key focus of debate and discussion in migration studies (Reynolds, 2010).

However, securitising spatially, these 'mezzo-level' migration studies for the most part, are located in British, Western European or North American countries, which limits the significance of this literature so far as it offers no considerations of the contexts like former Soviet Union (FSU), which has in the last twenty years, witnessed one of the greatest international migrations of the twentieth century. Between 1991 and 2000 an estimated nine million individuals left one country in this region and moved to live in another (ILO 2000)[17]. Thus, from a practical standpoint Central Asian countries' uneasy transition from a Soviet past, their now political environments, and their wide ranging ethnic distributions provide a special case study on whether social networking motivates and determines the migratory movement. The discourse in the present chapter seeks to locate the role of social capital into this phenomenon in Central Asia and introduce some insights into a processual approach to the relationship between the individual and the wider social and historical figurations of which they are part and to which they tend to live with.

In this respect we primarily focus on the ethnic migration networks in Central Asia and since the figurational approach looks to investigate the topic at hand as a process, it is necessary to provide a historical, contextual analysis of how the networks between ethnic populations emerge. Nonetheless, before going to articulate this discourse in a broader sense, we begin with a brief description of the research background that led to the materialization of this chapter.

Research Background

In the Central Asian context, research on migration has by and large emphasized on labour migration—what is classically understood as a rational decision made by an individual

---

[17] International Labour Organisation (2000) 'World Migration Tops 120 Million, Says ILO', press release, 2 March.

from a less developed situation to a more advantageous one after weighing risks and benefits or what are still generally categorized as 'push' or 'pull' factors. Based on empirical material derived from both primary and secondary sources, in this chapter however, we shall be seeking to build-on and complement the growing body of literature of third set called 'network' factors, which include free flow of information, transnational ethnic bonds, improved global communication and transnational familial networks etc. While network factors are not a direct cause of migration they do however, facilitate it.

For primary sources, qualitative interviews were undertaken in Uzbekistan and Russia in 2011 and 2012. Some fifteen qualitative interviews took place with young people and their parents of Uzbek nationality and citizenship. This was over a period of two months. The sample was drawn from Tashkent (Uzbekistan) and Moscow (Russia). Given the specific nature of the research criteria, access to the research sample was achieved through a 'snowball' method. The participants ranged from nineteen to thirty five years old, and involved a sample of five women and ten men. Although the analysis is based on the views and experiences of all of those interviewed in the respective research sites of Uzbekistan and Russia, for illustrative purposes we highlight the interviews, which took place with twelve participants with Uzbek nationality and citizenship.

The main objective of the research has been to explore the ethnic migratory flows in post-Soviet Central Asia and how transnational ethnic and kinship bonds operate in the migratory movements of Russian minority people in Uzbekistan and play a role for resource mobilization and facilitation of migratory flows.

In the analysis of firsthand empirical material, social capital is viewed as an important social resource in the process of migration; however, whilst social capital has been constructed in alternative ways by different authors, as Anne Kovalainen sees the inherent appeal of social capital as that it is at one and the same time an economic, a political and a sociological concept, giving it interdisciplinary prominence and potential (Kovalainen, 2004: 157); we work with a broad understanding of the concept that covers features of social life—networks, norms and trust—that enable participants to act together more effectively to pursue shared objectives (Putnam, 1995b: 664-665). Considerably, in this respect, there happens to be an extension and a broadening of the range of the content of the concept: from the level of organisations (or mezzo-level) to that of social life as a whole (or macro-level). Nevertheless, the latter came to include cities, regions and even whole countries, as the referent is to social life in general. Thus, such a conceptualisation of social capital can do the 'bonding,' 'bridging' or even 'linking' of social groups (Koniordos, 2008). As the first form, 'bonding', is related to the ties between people who are in similar situations, has an exclusive character and is oriented towards the inner part of a social group. The second, 'bridging,' links people in different situations, who belong to different social groups (Svendsen 2006), and has a comprehensive character.

Figurational Shifts and Migratory Flows in post Soviet Central Asia

While it is difficult to summarize the data that led to the identification of changing connotations and expectations of the populations in Central Asia, it is more daunting to demonstrate the figurational shifts in the region. Essentially, we argue that since the fall of Soviet Union the network of mutual dependencies between people in Central Asia became more extensive and intensive, for instance diaspora relations, back home support, return migration facilities etc. emerged increasingly. This region became more entangled in wider figurations on a global level. People were increasingly subject to a greater variety of social pressures to adjust their actions to new social relations. Indeed every individual, especially senior citizens are necessarily fully aware of these new pressures, but the growing complexity between more and more people generate new models of conduct that develop and gradually diffuse throughout the population. Herein, we do only briefly refer to the kind of evidence that represent this growing social complexity and consequences thereof. The indicators of this change are often quantitative indices such as population statistics, so herein the figurational approach adopts a 'multi-methods' strategy.

After the collapse of the Soviet Union in December 1991 and the abandoning of strict state regulation of population movement, the newly independent Central Asian countries have experienced significant fluctuation in population movement

(Abazov, 1999). In particular, amidst the political changes that swept throughout Central Asia, the right to migrate was synonymous in the minds of many with the establishment of democracy. A mosaic of networks and migration patterns (ethnically based migrations, return migration, labour migration, transit migration) gathered pace during the 1990s throughout the region and was further inflated by huge numbers of refugees, asylum-seekers and displaced persons as conflict and war broke out in different areas, notably in the Caucasus and south-east Europe (Tonelli, 2003).

Between 1991 and 2000 an estimated nine million individuals left one county in the post Soviet Central Asia and moved to live in another.[18] This mass migration has affected the political, economic and social development of the countries involved, not to mention the lives of many individuals and groups (Randitz, 2006). Specifically the economic dwindling, with the collapse of Communism and the consequent decline of the overall standards of life among general masses have not only intensified the pressure on labour migration and new networks, but the collapse of effective control along extensive land borders and an explosion in irregular migration (see Marat, 2009). Such a major event in world history has not escaped the considerations of scholars, who have studied this process. Yet, there are still many accounts to tell about this post Soviet experiment and its ramifications for groups and individuals, like the collapse

---

[18] International Labour Organisation (2000) 'World Migration Tops 120 Million, Says ILO', press release, 2 March.

of the Soviet Union left scores of labour migrants and their families stuck in a country where they unexpectedly happen to be the minority, and immersed them with a multitude of possible 'push' factors, or compulsions to rediscover historical ethnic networks to migrate to their home land.

Kyrgyzstan, the population of which in 1991 was 4.5 million, is a good example of the mobility of people in Central Asia. As per official figures, the net migration from the country for the years from 1989 until 1994 was 339600 people or 7.5 percent of its entire population.[19] Other sources put it to 13.1 percent of the total population of Kyrgyzstan.[20] Rather similar has been the case in other core Central Asian countries and of the all, ethnic migration has been the major issue. In Uzbekistan for instance, before independence, 60 percent of the population of Tashkent, was Russians. By 1993, Russians make up just 40 percent of Tashkent's population.[21] On the whole Russian population in Uzbekistan declined from 8.3 percent in 1989 to 5.6 percent in 1996. Tatars also left Uzbekistan: between 1989 and 1996, their number dwindled from 657,000 to 343,000.[22] Following table offers a solid sense in this respect.

---

[19] *CIS Migration Report*. 1996. Geneva: IOM, pp. 66-67.

[20] *Slovo Kyrgyzstana*. 1995. (5 January).

[21] "The Russians Say Goodbye to All That," The Economist, (328) 7827: 38 (Sept 4, 1993).

[22] Tim Heleniak. 1997. The Changing Nationality Composition of the Central Asian and Trans-Caucasian States. *Post-Soviet Geography and Economics,* 38 (6): 373.

Table: 8.1 Population Change due to Migration in Central Asia by Ethnicity (1989-1996)

Country/Ethnicity	Year/Percent (%)		
	1989	1996	1999-2000
Uzbekistan			-
Uzbeks	71.0	76.6	-
Russians	8.3	5.6	3.00
Tatars	3.3	1.5	-
Jews	0.5	0.1	-
Germans	0.2	0.1	-
Others	16.7	16.3	-
Kyrgyzstan			
Kyrgyz	52.0	59.9	-
Russian	21.4	15.6	12.5
Uzbek	12.8	14.1	-
Ukrainians	2.5	1.6	-
Germans	2.4	0.5	-
Jews	0.1	00	-
Others	8.9	8.3	-
Tajikistan			
Tajiks	62.1	68.1	-
Uzbeks	23.4	24.4	-
Russians	7.6	3.4	1.00
Others	6.9	4.1	-
Turkmenistan			
Turkmen	72.0	75.4	-
Russians	9.5	6.6	2.00
Others	18.5	18.0	-

Kazakhstan

Kazaks	39.5	47	-
Russians	37.7	33.9	30.0
Germans	5.8	2.6	-
Others	17.0	16.4	-

Source: Tim Heleniak, (1997), Peyrouse, (2008: 4) (for full detail see references).

Thus, revealed from the above table is that Russians comprised near about 20 percent of the total population of these five states: roughly 9.5 million people in 1989. However, their presence was not equably spread in these countries, which consequently led these States to face a unique domestic situation. While the titular population dominated in Uzbekistan, Turkmenistan, and Tajikistan; Kyrgyzstan and Kazakhstan were home to large non-titular minorities. The Kyrgyz accounted for only 65 percent of the population of their republic. The Kazakhs would not cross the majority threshold until the 1999 census (53 percent of the population). Albeit, their status were varied, these States however, had to deal with a similar dilemma: how to affirm a "de-Russified" national identity in the wake of local economic collapse, which crop up as bonds among the former Soviet republics collapsed, and how to do so without integrating into the larger post-Soviet space (Peyrouse, 2008).

Ethnicity in Central Asia was one of the major spheres, wherein the content of de-Russification was expressed. This process however has not been without predicaments and implicitly or explicitly, underlined irredentism, ethnic conflict, ethnic cleansing, and consequently mass ethnic migration.

Still, however, one must not lost sight of the broader post-Soviet socio-economic and politico-cultural context in which such mass ethnic migration and consequent figurations occurred.

Contextual View of Ethnic Migratory Flows

After the collapse of Soviet Union, the Central Asian states experienced widely divergent transitions to democracy. While Tajikistan experienced long-term instability following the end of its civil war in 1997; the situation in Kazakhstan, Uzbekistan and Turkmenistan and Kyrgyzstan was also relatively instable. The Ferghana Valley in particular remains a source of instability within the region, accompanied by the ongoing conflict in Afghanistan, which spills over into Central Asia in several ways. Specifically in Ferghana Valley, which is a large and densely-populated region divided between Kyrgyzstan, Tajikistan and Uzbekistan, a high level of xenophobia toward ethnic minorities is prevalent and inter-ethnic tensions are strong. Indeed, huge governance challenges still persist in whole Central Asia. Corruption is rife and patronage systems dictate the allocation of local resources. In 2010, Transparency International ranked Uzbekistan, Turkmenistan and Kyrgyzstan within the top 15 most corrupt countries, with Uzbekistan and Turkmenistan ranking 172 out 178, and Kyrgyzstan ranking 164 out of 178. Tajikistan ranked 154, and Kazakhstan ranked 105. Specifically, political co-operation between and among

Central Asian states on migration issues remain insufficient (IOM, 2011) and the transition to a market economy is yet challenged in some states like Uzbekistan and is complicated by high unemployment and the collapse of the industries.

In this backyard the poverty remains a serious issue in Central Asia. For instance 51 percent of the Kyrgyz population lives below the national poverty line, as do 34.6 percent of Kazakh citizens and 26.5 percent of the Uzbeks. Forty four percent of Turkmen live on less than $2 a day.[23] To somewhat similar stand in 2009, the percentage of population living on less than two dollars a day was 50 percent or greater in every Central Asian country except Kazakhstan. Such a social context in Central Asia added by ever-day nationalism, which includes language politics and redefining of history and cultural symbols (Light 2011) has proven particularly difficult for marginalized groups, including ethnic minorities, because the status of a minority in a nationalising state is not as straightforward as it seems on the surface—it is fraught with ambiguities.

Under such circumstances the set of choices available to a minority trapped in a post-Soviet nationalising state as defined by Laitin (1998:158) are: exit, voice and loyalty-with arms. Among these alternatives, exit or more precisely emigration or return migration is widely desired. Scott Randitz (2006) study solidly confirms this stance, wherein it is reported that the most common reason for desiring to

---

[23] United Nations Development Programme, "Human Development Report 2002." Online available from: http://hdr.undp.org/ reports/ global/2002/en (Accessed September 12, 20011).

leave among minority people in Central Asia are economic problems or 'low standard of living' and 'prospects for their children.'

Thus the motivations for departure and to relocate their-selves to historical figurations are multiple among minorities, and pose at the same time economic, social, and cultural concerns, but the political, which includes post-Soviet nationalising state, carried out in each republic provided a strong impetus among minorities to emigrate. Absence of official support, the strong feelings that especially Russian minorities hold toward Central Asian education system, which they perceive useless and gives impetus to the principal cause of emigration i.e. absence of a future, or the perception of such, for the younger generations and the degradation of the education system. According to some recent surveys, the proportion of individuals who wanted to emigrate was much higher—43 percent in Uzbekistan, 36 percent in Kyrgyzstan, 66 percent in Tajikistan—mainly to provide a future for their children. Among the specified cause the medium of instruction in schools has been the predominant (Peyrouse, 2008).

Nevertheless, such circumstances influenced migration decisions of minorities, not only insofar as it affected their material well being, but as Lebedeva (1997) holds that about one-quarter of the Russians in Kazakhstan and about one-third of those in Uzbekistan thought that to be Russian meant to live in Russia. They presented the Russian language and culture as more important elements of identification. More than half affirmed Russia as the land of their ancestors, *otechestvo*, more than a quarter defined it as their motherland, *rodina* (Lebedeva, 1997:60-61). Thus the continuum of identity and the multiplicity of definitions of self with Russia are still there in Central Asia (Poppe and Hagendoom, 2001: 57-71). In fact in Kazakhstan, according to data from the Moscow institute INDEM, 24 percent of Russians still regard themselves as citizens of the Soviet Union in 1998. Even at the end of the 1990s, 23 percent of the Russians in Uzbekistan continued to see themselves as either Soviet or stateless.[24] In a sense this continuum of identity is what represents an example of what Nobert Elias calls a figuration—the web of interdependences formed among human beings and which connects them: that is to say, a network of mutually oriented and dependent persons (1990:249). In what follows we have attempted to locate the transnational longing and belonging among Russian ethnic minority in Uzbekistan and their migratory flows within the web of figurational interdependences formed over time.

Transnational Social Networks and Ethnic Migration in Post-Soviet Uzbekistan

The concepts of Ethnicity and social networks have in recent times attracted much public attention and have influenced public policy debates in contemporary sociology

---

[24] Vendina, I. 2001. "Russkie v stranakh byvshevo SSSR." Online available from: (Accessed 18 April 2010)

and elsewhere. Yet, ethnicity seems to have received a limited and problematic attention in the mainstream migration studies and this has been more in the context of former Soviet Union. As discussed earlier that migration is classically understood as a rational decision made by an individual from a less developed situation to a more advantageous one after weighing risks and benefits or what are still generally categorized as 'push' or 'pull' factors. Theories accounting migration process in the Central Asia also tend to borrow from both sides of the structure—agency dichotomy whilst emphasising either 'push' or 'pull' factors, but miss to articulate the 'network factor' or broader conceptualisation of social capital in this process. Rather there are some accounts (e.g. Randitz et al. 2009) which suggest that increased political authoritarianism and a high police presence in this region discourages people including minorities from extensively interacting, which cement citizens to their pre-existing social circles and thus limits their potential of developing new networks. In this connection however, our field interviews in Uzbekistan and Russia contend this assertion by demonstrating particular ways in which transnational ethnic groups create similar networks of trust and reciprocity across geographical neighbourhoods and nation states, which implicitly or explicitly help facilitate the migratory flow. For instance

Bronislav (name changed), father of two kids, who belong to Russian minority in Uzbekistan hold that:

> I know that I'm Uzbek, because that's what it writes on my qualification certificates, my passport and I know that I'm not really Russian in the sense that I wasn't born out there but I still choose to identify culturally with them because my grandparents were Russian and still everything is done in a Russian style at home and so it's what I feel more comfortable associating myself with them [. . . .] In fact we still have some tertiary relatives there in Moscow and last time I was for some two years there (Moscow) working in a garment industry and during that time my relatives, whom I'd never seen before, facilitated my stay in a small city some 80 miles away from the Moscow city. I would say, without their (relatives) help it would have been quite worrying, but their presence made me feel at home (interview location: Uzbekistan, October 2011).

This narrative confirms some existing body of literature in the context of Central Asia (e.g. Kılavuz, 2009), which suggests that local and regional allegiances are important determinants of identity in Uzbekistan and Central Asia at large. Today, people from different regions of Uzbekistan see themselves as distinct groups and (but the same ethnic group) differentiate themselves through dialect, traditions, and customs, and even after three generations, they identify with the region of their paternal grandfather's origin. Popular belief holds that in order to identify with a region, one's ancestors must have lived there for at least three generations. Indeed when asked where they are from, majority of respondents in our study generally gave their grandfather's place of origin rather than their own birthplace, when these are different. And as revealed herein this continuum of identity definitions in one or other way are associated with the migratory movements as one of our participants highlighted that:

> I would say my family is important to me. They give me my cultural identity, my Russian identity, my Russian-ness, and this is what helped me in my life-course trajectories, because not only tertiary relatives or friends of friends, but my ethnicity and cultural identity were often key facilitators in my migration strategies to Russia. You know just knowing that they're out there supporting me, helping me to understand who I am (interview location: Uzbekistan October 2011).

Actually Veniamin (name changed), a young, single interviewee came to Russia in 2007 for studies. He no longer had any rapport there in Moscow and his first six months in Russia were quite tricky. However, in the meantime he got to share a flat with some Russian students, few of whose parents or grandparents had been to Uzbekistan in Soviet times, but had returned to Russia after the collapse of Soviet Union. After discovering some ethnic and historical similarities Veniamin came to be treated as an actual member of that Russian students group and they proved an important source of practical support for him, lending him money whenever he was in need. Veniamin is now a full-time student, living residence halls at his university. At the time of interview however he was back home for a month and was having close contacts with his friends in Russia, having online chat every day with his Russian friends.

> Oh! Exactly I thank God, I've Internet at my home [. . .] It makes such a massive difference having that, feeling a part of your friends' lives back home. Photos, college pictures, club memories whatever . . . (Interview location: Uzbekistan October 2011)

Indeed with the help of his Russian friends . . . has attained enough confidence to help facilitate the migratory strategies of four of his Uzbek friends to Russia for job purposes.

A similar case has been with Demyan (name changed) when he was in Russia for 12 years, working as a business man. His case revealed that some already existing networks and ethnic background helped him a lot in establishing a business unit in Moscow. As of now Demyan has established good social connections in Moscow and helped many of his relatives and friends to migrate and settle in many regions of Russia:

> I have made connections with a couple of businessmen and educators in Russia in case I should find myself moving back at some point in the future or send my kids for studies. I've good relationships with them and even they call me when they require any help or come to Uzbekistan.

Such evidences reflects the role of 'ethnicity utility' by which we mean the social support available through networks that are connected to the ancestors place of residence and this discourse implicitly or explicitly identifies social capital as one form of remittance that migrants transfer between their country of residence and country of origin. The literature on trans-nationalism also suggest this viewpoint by highlighting the many ways in which skills and resources are mobilised by family, kin or ethnic groups to sustain networks and social capital across national borders (see Goulbourne, 2002; Zontini, 2004b). Even trans-nationalism reflects the 'sustained ties of persons, networks and organisations across the borders across multiple nation-states' (Faist, 2000: 190). As such, trans-nationalism does not mean the loss of social capital but rather its recreation in new and diverse forms. For example

Aleksey—a 31 year old, who works as a manager in Russia, holds that:

> Being ethnically Russian means you're definitely more at an advantage in Moscow because your identity gets you through in many ways. I've been in Russia for last eight years and feel like at home and people around give me a due say and crave to be my friend. Yet I've not forgotten my Uzbek friends my relatives. My brother lives in Tashkent and we're in contact every night. If we don't make phone call then we're on the Internet, messaging each other. Luckily my business means I'm coming back to Uzbekistan every five to six months, so I keep up with my friends there and I don't feel like I'm missing out and it's so effortless and easy to send a email just to say "Hi how are U?" I' do always persuade my brother and my friends to come out and see me and they do. At least I do come here every summer. I have quite a network of people in Russia and Uzbekistan to call on when I need it. In fact I helped my cousins to find good lucrative jobs in Moscow and arranged accommodation for them, otherwise they were hesitating to come to Russia (Interview location: Uzbekistan October 2011).

On the whole our data suggests how immigrants depend on networks and solidarity ties (social capital) in order to sustain their transnational activities and help facilitate and motivate even those to migrate, who otherwise hesitate to migrate to a new land by reducing cost and risk. And all through this process ethnicity play a key role. Such evidence also confirms findings of Agadjanian et al. (2008) study in Kyrgyzstan, wherein it is demonstrated that migration-related social capital retains a strong impact, but having close kin abroad has a stronger effect among Europeans while having a network partner intending to migrate has a stronger impact on the degree of migration intentions among Asians.

However, in the context of Central Asia as said earlier the massive departures of the 1990s deeply affected the Russian communities of the various republics. The migrations separated families, weakened social networks, and left the remaining Russians feeling disaffected and discomforted. But thanks to contemporary ITCs, the extensive use of which constitutes a fairly new dimension in the study of migration and diasporic communities that has recently begun attracting the attention of scholars from a variety of disciplines and methodologies. This is still very much an under-researched area, particularly regarding the study of the use of ICTs by migrants within Europe. It may be in this backdrop that Borkert *et al.* (2009:25) proposed the 'establishment of a European Research Area on ICT and migrations' especially regarding the use of new technologies by immigrants and ethnic minorities.

Still, this is not all about the post-collapse of Soviet Union and consequent transitions. There are many stories to tell about this crossroads of transition and its ramifications for groups and individuals. In what follows we shall be pondering over some of the major nuisances that emerge out the migratory processes in Central Asia.

Gender Stereotype, Migration and Social Security of Women in Central Asia

Women constitute half of the world's population, perform nearly two-thirds of the work, receive one-tenth of the world's income and own less than one-hundredth of the world's property (UNDP, 2003). Undoubtedly the matter is more serious in the context of Central Asia, where the process of feminization of poverty is intimately connected to the cultural and institutional limitations that put a ceiling on women's involvement in economic activity (see Bhat, 2011). An old Kyrgyz saying 'a frog-headed [stupid] man is better than a golden-headed [intelligent] woman,' is tempting to suggest that the proverb reflects the overall attitude towards women in Central Asia (Saidazimova, 2005).

Women in Central Asia, thus for the most part, get less of the material resources, social status, power and opportunities for self-actualization than men do. Global migration has further added to this relegation by leaving many women at risk. The left-behind women of Central Asia are one example, where the concern assumes special meaning in view of the fact that the incidence of women-headed households[25] is on the increase for various reasons in Central Asia (Mittra and Kumar, 2004: 202-3), entailing widowhood, separation, desertion, non-absorption of widowed daughters-in-law by husbands' families. By all probability, We would argue that this scenario of women in Central Asia is more specifically due to high rate of male migration to Russia and other European countries. Although no study has extensively investigated how labour migration affects the women left behind. However, as David Trilling (2009:84) exclusively demonstrates 'single women are abundant in Tajikistan, where more than half the working-age male population is abroad,' the left-behind women are more susceptible to social, mental and physical insecurity. International Organization for Migration (2011) report on *Central Asia Operational Strategy 2011-2015,* reveals that in Central Asia, labour migration of males has created a significant number of female-headed households. These households are more vulnerable to serious poverty and to social exclusion. In Kyrgyzstan, for instance the poverty and vulnerability rate among households headed by women is at 58.7 percent. To somewhat similarly in Kazakhstan, the poverty and vulnerability rate among households headed by women is at 31.3 percent. However, in Kazakhstan the data is of urban areas excluding rural, where rates might be much higher (Dang, 2009:41).

---

[25] United Nations Human Settlements Programme (UN-HABITAT) (2008) report on *State of the World's Cities,* reveals that in the cities of Central Asia, woman-headed households are almost the norm, rather than the exception.

Abandonment of families is thus, a growing problem—men engage in labour migration, but do not return home, leaving their wives and children in poverty and hardship. Even some migrants return home, but having lost money, some fall prey to human traffickers. Particularly migrants from the Caucasus and Central Asia, who work in Russia are invariably paid less than locals (see European Commission, 2003), some dismissed at anytime without pay for any reason, and have no redress and still some like that:

> Most Tajik migrants who die in Russia are not victims
> of racism, but of deadly accidents at the workplace.
> Every single train coming back from Russia carries
> coffins and mutilated people (Tajik sociologist).[26]

Poverty, Women Migration and the Risks upon

Today, women constitute almost half of all international migrants worldwide—around 95 million (UNFPA, 2006). Equally in Central Asia, women comprise half of the (total between 60-90 percent) labour migrants from Tajikistan and Uzbekistan, although most half of the female labour migrants are from Kyrgyzstan, travelling to Russia and Kazakhstan, which increased annually until 2008. Yet, despite their contributions to poverty reduction and struggling economies,

---

[26] Interview with a Tajik sociologist, Saodat Olimova, documented in: ICG (International Crisis Group). 2003. *Youth in Central Asia: Losing the New Generation.* Asia Report N°66, Osh: Brussels, p. 33.

it is only recently that the international community has begun to grasp the significance of what migrant women have to offer. And it is only recently that policymakers are acknowledging the particular challenges and risks women confront when venturing into new lands.

It is often said that migrant labour fills the 'three-D' jobs: dirty, degrading and dangerous. Research in Southern [and Eastern] European countries demonstrates the extent to which the migrants take jobs that the locals refuse. It is simply a matter of proxy (Reynieri, 2001) which arguably for the most part is substituted by women migrant, who therefore, come at the cost.

In this backdrop, as discussed earlier that women in Central Asia get less of the material resources, social status, power and opportunities for self-actualization, the *Protocol to Prevent, Suppress and Punish Trafficking in Persons, especially Women and Children, Supplementing the U.N. Convention Against Transnational Organized Crime* (2000) identifies 'poverty, underdevelopment, and lack of equal opportunity' as some of the 'factors that make persons, especially women, vulnerable to social and physical insecurity.' In fact, poverty, and in particular the 'feminization of poverty,' is often identified as a risk factor for, or root cause of trafficking. Undeniably in Central Asia one of the most common forms of trafficking in person concerns the trafficking of women for prostitution or sexual exploitation. There is considerable evidence (see Castles, 2003; Jackson, 2006; Marat 2009) that human trafficking victims in Central Asia are often brought into their situation by recruiters—men or women, who promise jobs and financial stability to women in poverty. These recruiters, employed by traffickers, tend to be known to the victim, often taking the form of formerly trustworthy roles such as relatives or friends (Eason, 2011).

Thus under the label of job promise and financial stability, the trafficking of women in the former Soviet Union is rife. Such predicaments however, seem directly linked to the overall socio-economic, political and porous border scenario of these countries. For example in 2005 in Tajikistan an estimated 40 percent of the population was unemployed and 64 percent was living in poverty (Haarr, 2007:268). Roughly in the same and subsequent years, the most cases of families selling their virgin daughters to the Gulf States for $2,000-3,000 have been recorded in Tajikistan (Marat, 2009:39). Equally the 2009 *Trafficking in Person Report* shows Uzbekistan as a source country of women and girls trafficked to USA, UAE, Japan, Israel and India etc (US Department of State). Scrutinizing the causes, poverty, unemployment and unawareness, and existence of organised crime rings are predominant in Uzbekistan and Central Asia at large. Robustly this whole phenomenon in Central Asia is found at the nexus of globalisation and migration.

Concluding Remarks

Globalisation couples extra intricacy to the relationship between poverty, migration and trafficking of women in Central Asia, by fabricating uncertainty for women, who find it harder to support themselves and their families and are pressed to hunt for employment, even if beyond their borders. However, in seeking this, women in Central Asia are more likely to accept the greater risks in taking on more dangerous or precarious work, and in migrating under insecure conditions from rural areas to globalised urban centres and abroad. In those cases where the conditions under which migration occurs are dangerous, women may be more likely to be trafficked or at times used as channels of weapon smuggling, which needs to be perceived as a threat to global security, because it is often part of a larger phenomenon of illegal migration and transnational organized crime that is believed to threaten global governance and states around the world. We are indeed stand facing with a perplexed state of affairs, wherein security and humanitarian considerations, immigration and asylum, undocumented migration and human trafficking, criminal and victim, and national and human securities statuses get intractably amalgamated. But not too late for political scientists, Sovietologists, transitologists, demographers and sociologists in general, who have so far all proven slow to carefully analyze and interpret the current evolutions of migration policies in post Soviet space and work out some sound mechanisms.

Moreover, theories accounting migratory flows in the Central Asia tend to locate the reasons encouraging an individual to migrate into the classical structure—agency dichotomy whilst emphasising either 'push' or 'pull' factors, and so is true of ethnic migratory flows. However, the findings discussed in this chapter suggest that the contextualized meanings around notions of identity, home and cultural belonging and the consequent social networks are also central to understanding the experiences of ethnic migrants in Central Asia, which implicitly or explicitly constitute a third set called 'network' factors. While network factors are not a direct cause of migration they do however, facilitate it by providing sponsorship, patronage, credit, or advice through social connections that emerge out of the already established trust in the community.

Our data reveals that the migrants recognised that shared ethnic bonds in Russia provided them a feasible context to develop more and more social capital, and valued the 'taken for granted' aspect of their same ethnic friendships, as well as the common understanding that emerged from this. These experiences led many to illustrate that the family are important to them in constructing their ethnic identity. Together with these evidences have implications not just for understanding migration in Central Asia, but also how family migrations, ethnic networks and transnational relationships need to be theorized, conceptualized and researched. For that reason, there is a need to combine 'push', 'pull' and 'network factor' perspectives to gain a fuller picture of the interconnections, negotiations, and dynamics of migratory flows in Central Asia over time. Specifically migration, internet, social networking and diasporas' is an interdisciplinary collection that stands to be examined in the context of Central Asia, because that explores new emerging media and technological networks developed between those who have migrated and those who have stayed in place. This position focuses on transactions, which as our interviews revealed also facilitate migratory flows and help to construct transnational and diasporic communities. An additional tenet is to make use of so-called mobile methods by studying transnational, interpersonal and organizational networks (Bu¨scher, Urry and Witchger 2010). However, 'networks' should not mean purely *social* networks since the 'convergence of social evolution and information technologies has created a new material basis for the performance of activities throughout the social structure. Yet networks are to be viewed as dynamic open structures, so long as they are able to effect communication with new nodes and to innovate (Castells 1996: 470-1). Networks can't be isolated or frozen in time and explained outside of their temporal context, because they have actually developed over time and therefore in order to understand them, they need to be examined as flows.

Such a line of investigation is proposed so that we do justice to the complexity or 'messy nature' of the phenomena of migration in post-Soviet Central Asia rather than try to over-simplify the process into more easily manageable, compartmentalised, dichotomous ways of looking.

BIBLIOGRAPHY

Abazov, R. (1999). Economic Migration in Post-Soviet Central Asia: The Case of Kyrgyzstan. *Post-Communist Economies*, 11 (2): 237-252.

Adams, L. (1999). Invention, Institutionalisation and Renewal in Uzbekistan's National Culture. *European Journal of Cultural Studies* 2 (3): 355-73.

Adams, M. (2006). 'Hybridising Habitus and Reflexivity: Towards an Understanding of Contemporary Identity'. *Sociology, 40(3)*: 511-28.

Agadjanian, V., Nedoluzhko, L and Kumskov, G. (2008). Eager to Leave? Intentions to Migrate Abroad among Young People in Kyrgyzstan. *International Migration Review,* 42 (3): 620-653.

Ahuja, R. (1997). *Social Problems in India,* 2nd Edition. Jaipur: Rawat Publications.

Aminov, K., Jensen, V., Juraev, S., Overland, I., Tyan, D. and Uulu, Y. (2010). Language Use and Language Policy in Central Asia. *Central Asia Regional Data Review,* 2 (1): 1-29.

Aries, E. and Seider M. (2005). 'The Interactive Relationships between Class Identity and the College Experience: The Case of Lower Income Students'. *Qualitative Sociology,* 28(4): 419-93.

Babar, Stingler, Perry, *et al.,* (2010). Tobacco-use psychosocial risk profiles of girls and boys in urban India: Implications for gender-specific tobacco intervention development. *Nicotine and Tobacco Research.* Vol. 12 (1), pp. 29-36.

Baskakova, M. (2007). *Some Aspects of Youth Education, Gender Equality and Employment in Caucasus and Central Asia.* Moscow: ILO.

Beck, U. (1992). *Risk Society: Towards a New Modernity.* London: Sage.

Beck, U. (1994). *The Reinvention of Politics: Towards a Theory of Reflexive Modernisation.* Cambridge: Polity Press.

Beck, U. (2002). 'Zombie Categories: Interview with Ulrich Beck'. *In:* U. Beck and E. Beck-Gernsheim (Eds.) *Individualisation* (pp. 202-13). London: Sage.

Beck, U. and Beck-Gernsheim, E. (Eds.) (2002). *Individualisation.* London: Sage.

Becker, G. (1964) *Human Capital.* New York: National Bureau of Economic Research.

Beck-Gernsheim, E. (1996). 'Life is a Planning Project'. *In:* S. Lash, B. Szerszynski and B. Wynne (Eds.) *Risk, Environment and Modernity: Towards a New Ecology* (pp. 106-39). London: Sage.

Bennett, T., Emmison, M. and Frow, J. (1999). *Accounting for Tastes: Australian Everyday Culture.* Cambridge: University Press.

Bertolote, M and Fleischmann, A. (2002). Suicide and psychiatric diagnosis: A worldwide perspective. *World Psychiatry,* 1, 181-185.

Bhaduri, A. (2008). *Growth and employment in the era of globalisation: Some lessons from the Indian experience.* New Delhi: ILO, Sub-regional Office for South Asia.

Bhat, B. (2011). Gender earnings and poverty reduction: post-Communist Uzbekistan. *Journal of Asian and African Studies,* 1-21: DOI: 10.1177/0021909611407584.

Bhat, M. Aslam (2013). Revisiting the Youth Corridor: From Classical through Post-modern to Late-modern Sociology. *International Review of Sociology: Revue Internationale de Sociologie,* 23(1): 200-20.

Bhat, M. Aslam and Rather, T. Ahmad (2012). Socio-Economic Factors and Mental Health of Young People in India and China: An Elusive Link with Globalisation. *Asian Social Work and Policy Review,* 6(1): 1-22.

Bhavsar, V and Bhugra, D. (2008). Globalisation: Mental health and social economic factors. *Global Social Policy,* 8 (3), 378-96.

Bhugra, D and Mastrogianni, A. (2004). Globalisation and mental disorders: Overview with relation to depression. *The British Journal of Psychiatry,* 184, 10-20.

Bian, Y. (2002). Chinese social stratification and social mobility. *Annual Review of Sociology, 28,* 91-116.

Bibeau, G. (1997). Cultural psychiatry in a creolizing world: Questions for a new research agenda. *Transcultural Psychiatry*, 34, 9-41.

Boasu, I. (2004). *The faces of globalisation: A dilemma for India* [online]. Retrieved from: http://www.spacedaily.com/news/india-04e.html

Borkert, M., Cingolani, P. and Premazzi, V. (2009). *The State of the Art of Research in the EU on the Uptake and Use of ICT by Immigrants and Ethnic Minorities (IEM).* Luxembourg: Office for Official Publications of the European Communities.

Bottrell, D. (2009). 'Dealing with Disadvantage: Resilience and the Social Capital of Young People's Networks'. *Youth and Society, 40 (4)*: 476-501.

Bourdieu, P. (1977). *Outline of a Theory of Practice.* New York: Cambridge University Press.

Bourdieu, P. (1984). 'Distinction: A Social Critique of the Judgement of Taste'. In W. Malcolm (Ed.) *Modern Sociological Theory* (pp. 198-202).Sage: London.

Bourdieu, P. (1986). 'The Forms of Capital'. *In:* J. Richardson (Ed.) *Handbook of Theory and Research on the Sociology of Education* (pp. 241-58). New York: Greenwood.

Bourdieu, P. (1996) *State Nobility.* Cambridge: Polity Press.

Bourdieu, P. (2004) 'The Forms of Capital'. *In:* S. Ball (Eds.) *The Routledge Flamer Reader in Sociology of Education* (pp. 15-29).London: Routledge Flamer.

Bourdieu, P. (1986). 'The Forms of Capital'. *In:* J. Richardson (Eds.), *Handbook of Theory and Research for the Sociology of Education*. New York: Greenwood, pp. 241—258.

Brannen, Julia and Nilsen, Ann (2002) 'Young Peoples' Time Perspectives: From Youth to Adulthood', *Sociology,* 36(3): 513-37.

Brannen, Julia and Nilsen, Ann. (2005) 'Individualisation, Choice and Structure: A Discussion of Current Trends in Sociological Analysis'. *The Sociological Review,* 53(3):412-28.

Broaded, C. (1983). Higher education policy changes and stratification in China. *China Quarterly, 93,* 125—41.

Brown, B., Larson, R and Sarswahi, T. (2002). *The worlds youth: Adolescence in eight regions of the globe.* Cambridge: Cambridge University Press.

Brown, D. (2005). Protecting workers: Health and safety in the globalizing economy through international trade treaties. *International Journal of Occupational and Environmental Health,* 11 (2), 207-9.

Burdhan, P., Mookherjee, D and Tsumagari, M. (2009). *Middleman margins and globalisation.* Working Paper id: 2202. Retrieved from:

Carnoy, M. (2002). *Globalisation and educational restructuring.* Paris: International Institute of Educational Planning.

Carnoy, M., and Rhoten, D. (2002). What does globalisation mean for educational change? A comparative approach. *Comparative Education Review,* 46 (1), 1-9.

Castells, M. (1996). *The rise of the network society.* Blackwell: Oxford.

Castles, F. (2004). *The future of the welfare state.* Oxford: Oxford University Press.

Castles, S and Miller, J. (2003). *The Age of Migration.* New York: Guilford Press.

Castles, S. (2003). Towards a sociology of forced migration and social transformation. *Sociology,* **37**(1): 13-34.

Census (2011) *Provisional Population Totals Paper 1 of 2011: Jammu and Kashmir.* New Delhi: Office of the Registrar General and Census Commissioner India, Government of India.

Chan, J., and Pun, N. (2010). Suicide as protest for the new generation of Chinese migrant workers: Foxconn, global capital and the state. *The Asia-Pacific Journal: Japan Focus,* 8 (51), 2.

Chandrasekhar, C. P., Ghosh, J., and Roychowdhury. (2006). The demographic dividend and young India's economic future. *Economic and Political Weekly,* 41 (49), 5055-64.

Chao-R, K., (1994). Beyond parental control and authoritarian parenting style: Understanding Chinese parenting through the cultural notion of training. *Child Development,* 65, 1111-19.

Chao-R, K., and Stanley, S. (1996). Chinese parental influence and their children's school success: A paradox in the literature on parenting styles. In: Sing, L., ed. *Growing up the Chinese Way: Chinese Child and Adolescent*

Development, pp. 93-120. Hong Kong: The Chinese University Press.

Cheng, Y. (2010, March 10). Psychological issues raising among students. *China Daily.* Retrieved from: http:// Chinadaily.com.cn/index.html

China National Bureau of Statistics. (2006b). *Communiqué on major data of 1% national population sample survey in 2005.* Beijing: CNBS.

Chisholm, L. and du Bois-Reymond, M. (1993) 'Youth Transition, Gender and Social Change', *Sociology, 27(2)*: 259-79.

CIA (Central Intelligence Agency). (2009). *CIA World Factbook.* Available at: http://ww w.cia.gov/library/ publications/the-world-factbook/

Coleman, H., Gulyamova, J and Thomas, A. (2005). *National Development, Education and Language in Central Asia and Beyond.* Edited proceedings of the 6th International Language and Development Conference: 'Linguistic Challenges to National Development and International Co-operation.' Uzbekistan: British Council Uzbekistan.

Coleman, J. (1988) 'Social Capital in the Creation of Human Capital'. *American Journal of Sociology, 94(1)*:95-120.

Commonwealth Youth Programme. (1978). *Youth in Nation Building, Report of a Seychelles National Seminar*, London, Youth Division, Commonwealth Secretariat

Corrigall, J., Plagerson, S., Lund, C., and Myers. (2008). Global trade and mental health. *Global Social Policy*, 8 (3), 335-58.

Dang, R. (2009). Vulnerability to poverty in select Central Asian countries. *The European Journal of Comparative Economics,* **6** (1): 17-50.

Datta, D. (2008). *Teen suicides.* Retrieved from: http://indiatoday.Digitaltoday.in/cont entmail.php?option=com content&name=print&id=7170

De Young, J., Reeves, M. and Valyaeva, K. (2006). *Surviving the Transition? Case Studies of Schools and Schooling in the Kyrgyz Republic since Independence.* Greenwich: Information Age Publishing.

Deaton, A. (2002). Is world poverty falling? *Finance and Development,* 39 (2), 4-7.

Deb, S. (2001). A study on the negative effects of academic stress. Paper presented at the *International Seminar on Learning and Motivation,* Kedah Darul Aman: Malaysia.

Deb, S., Chatterjee, P., and Kerryann, W. (2010). Anxiety among high school students in India: Comparisons across gender, school type, social strata and perceptions of quality time with parents. *Australian Journal of Educational & Developmental Psychology,* 10, 18-31.

De-Brauw, A., and Rozelle, S. (2003). Returns to education in rural China. In: E. Hannum and A. Park ed. *Education and Reform in China.* Cambridge, MA: Harvard University Press.

Desjarlais, R., Eisenberg, L., Good, B., *et al.* (1995). *World mental health: Problems and priorities in low-income countries.* Oxford: Oxford University Press.

DeSouza, R. P., Kumar, S., and Shastri, S. (2009). *Indian Youth in the Transforming World.* Sage: Thousand Oaks, CA, USA.

Ding, Xueqin *et al.*, (1998). Physical activities and healthy mental development of youth-A survey and comparative study of the inducement of mental pressure among youth in Beijing and Hong Kong. *Journal of China Sports Science Society.* 5, [DOI]: cnki:SCN:11-3885.0.1998-05-02. Retrieved from: www.cnki.com.cn

District Statistics and Evaluation Agency. (2007). *Economic review 2006—07.* Leh: Directorate of Economics and Statistics Planning and Development. Pp. 26-27.

Dollar, D. (2001). Is globalisation good for your health. *Bulletin of the World Health Organisation*, 79, 832-833.

Dore, R. (1976) *The Diploma Disease: Education, Qualification and Development.* Berkeley: University of California Press.

Dunne, M. P., Sun, J., and Nguyen *et al.,* (2010). The influence of educational pressure on the mental health of adolescents in East Asia: Methods and tools for research. *Journal of Sciences.* Hue University, N0 61.

Dyson, J. (2006). 'Faces of the forest: children's work in the Indian Himalayas'. *In:* D. Behera. *Childhood in South Asia,* Oxford: Pearson Education, 32-51.

Dyson, J. (2008). Harvesting identities: youth, work and gender in the Indian Himalayas. *Annals of the Association of American Geographers,* 98, 160-79.

Eason, H. (2011). No recourse left: the impact of poverty on the resilience of women from the migrant-sending countries of Central Asia to Hiv/aids. *Resilience: Interdisciplinary Perspectives on Science and Humanitarianism* **1**(2): 86.

Edmunds J (2006) Migration studies: new directions? *Ethnicities,* **6**(4): 555-564.

Eduard, Glissant. (1997). *Poetics of relation.* Ann Arbor: University of Michigan Press.

EFI-Solar Foundation (Employers Federation of India, Indian Merchants Chamber). (2006). *Employment generation in post-globalisation era in greater mumbai.* EFI-Solar Foundation, Mumbai: India.

Eisenstadt, S.N. (1962). Archetypal patterns of youth. *Daedalus,* 91 (1), 28-46.

Elias, N. (1990). *O processo civilizador.* Translation by Ruy Jungmann. Rio de Janeiro: Jorge Zahar, v. 1.

Erikson, E. (1982). *The life cycle completed.* New York: Norton.

European Commission. (2003). *Report on the Functioning of the Transitional Arrangements Set Out in the 2003 Accession Treaty.* Brussels: European Commission.

Evans, K. (2007) 'Concepts of Bounded Agency in Education, Work and the Personal Lives of Young Adults'. *International Journal of Psychology, 42(2)*:85-93.

FAIST, T. (2000). *The Volume and Dynamics of International Migration and Transnational Social Spaces.* Oxford: Oxford University Press.

Fierman, W. (1995). Problems of Language law Implementation in Uzbekistan. *Nationalities Papers: The Journal of Nationalism and Ethnicity,* 23 (3): 573-595.

Fierman, W. (2009). Identity, Symbolism, and the Politics of Language in Central Asia. *Europe-Asia Studies,* 61(7): 1207-1228.

Forans, J and Bolin, G. (1995). *Youth Culture in Late Modernity,* London: Sage.

Froneberg, B. (2003). Psychological stress and well-being at work. *African Newsletter on Occupational Health and Safety,* 13 (2), 32-5.

Fuer, Lewis. (1969). *The conflict of generation: The character and significance of student movement.* London: Heinemmau Educated Books Ltd.

Furlong, A. and Cartmel, F. (1997) *Young People and Social Change: Individualisation and Risk Society in Late Modernity.* Buckingham: Open University Press.

GAATW (Global Alliance Against Traffic in Women). (2010). *Beyond Borders: Exploring Links between Trafficking, Globalisation, and Security.* GAATW and International Human Rights Clinic, Center for Human Rights and Global Justice, New York University School of Law, Pp.46.

George, V. (1998). Political ideology, globalisation and welfare futures in Europe. *Journal of Social Policy,* 27 (1), 17-36.

George, V., and Wilding P. (2002). *Globalisation and human welfare.* Houndmills: Palgrave.

Gergen, K. J. (1991). *The saturated self: Dilemmas of identity in contemporary life*. New York: Basic Books.

Ghaderi, R., Venkatesh, G., and Sampath, K. (2009). Depression, anxiety and stress among the Indian and Iranian students. *Journal of the Indian Academy of Applied Psychology,* 35 (1), 33-37.

Giddens, A. (1990). *The Consequences of Modernity.* Polity: Cambridge.

Giddens, A. (1991) *Modernity and Self-identity, Self and Society in the Late Modern Age.* Cambridge: Polity Press.

Giddens, A. (1994) 'Living in a Post-traditional Society'. In U. Beck, A. Giddens and S. Lash (Eds.) *Reflexive Modernization: Politics, Tradition and Aesthetics in the Modern Social Order* (pp. 56-109). Cambridge: Polity Press.

Giddens, A. (1999) *Runaway World: How Globalisation is Re-shaping Our Lives.* London: Profile Books.

Gilboy, George J., and Eric Heginbotham. (2004). The Latin Americanisation of China? *Current History*, 103 (674), 256.

Goldthrope, J. (1987) *Social Mobility and Class Structure.* Oxford: Clarendon Press.

Goldthrope, J. (1996) 'Class Analysis and the Reorientation of Class Theory: The Case of Persisting Differentials in Educational Attainments'. *British Journal of Sociology of Education, 47(3)*:481-505.

Goodall, k. Sarah. (2004). Rural to urban migration and urbanization in Leh Ladakh: A case study of three nomadic pastoral communities. *Mountain Research and Development*. Vol. 24 (3), pp. 220-227.

Goodkind, D., and West, L. A. (2002). China's floating population: Definitions, data and recent findings. *Urban Studies,* 39 (12), 2237-50.

Gore, M. S. (1977). *Indian Youth, Processes of Socialization,* Vishwa Yuvak Kendra New Delhi PP. 4-5.

Goulbourne, H. (2002). *Caribbean Transnational Experience*. London: Pluto Press.

Gupta, R. K., and Gupta Amita. (2006). *Concise encyclopaedia of India.* India: Atlantic Publishers and Distributors. Vol. 3, pp. 440-69.

Gururaj, G., & Isaac, M. K. (2001). *Epidemiology of suicides in Bangalore.* Bangalore: National Institute of Mental Health and Neuro Sciences, Publication No 43.

Haarr, R. (2007). Wife abuse in Tajikistan. *Feminist Criminology,* 2 (3): 245-270.

Harnois, G., and Gabriel, P. (2000). *Mental health and work: Impact issues and good practices*. Geneva: World Health Organisation.

Herman, H., and Jane-L., E. (2005). Mental health promotion in public health. *International Journal of Health Promotion and Education* (Supplement: The Evidence of Mental Health Promotion Effectiveness: Strategies for Action) 2, 42-6.

Hong, Y., and Li, X. (2007). Behavioural studies of female sex workers China: A literature and recommendations for research. In: Joseph, D., T. Dudley, L. Poston *et al., Gender Policy and HIV in China: Catalyzing Policy Change,* pp. 130-40. Springer: Publication.

Huber, E., and Stephens, J. D. (1998). Internationalisation and the social democratic welfare model: Crises and future prospects. *Comparative Political Studies,* 33 (3), 353-397.

Huber, E., and Stephens, J. D. (2001). *Partisan choice in global markets: Development and crisis of advanced welfare states.* Chicago: University of Chicago Press.

Humphrey, J. (2006). Prospects and challenges for growth and poverty reduction in Asia. *Development Policy Review,* 24 (1), 29-49.

ICG (International Crises Group). (2003). *Youth in central Asia: losing the new generation.* Brassek: ICG, 1.

ILO (International Labour Organization). (2006). *Global Employment Trends for Youth.* ILO-KILM Geneva, Switzerland.

India Today. (Feb 20, 2006). *Cover Story: Looking Ahead in Anger.* Pp. 12-57.

Ingrid, N., and Russell, S. (2006). *Job satisfaction and response to incentives among China's urban work force.* Department of Management, Working Paper Series 23/July 06 ISSN 1327-5216, Monash University.

Ingrid, N., and Russell, S. (2008). *Migration and social protection in China.* Singapore: World Scientific Publications, Pp. 265.

International Institute for Population Sciences (IIPS) and Population Council. (2010). *Youth in India: Situation and needs 2006-2007.* Mumbai: IIPS, Pp.73.

International Labour Organisation (ILO). (2002). *Globalisation and decent work in the Americas.* Geneva: ILO.

International Labour Organisation (ILO). (2006). *Globalisation and its effects on youth employment trends in Asia.* Paper presented to the Regional Expert Group Meeting on Development Challenges for Young People, Bangkok 28-30 March. Retrieved from: http://www.Globalpolicy.org/globaliz/econ/2003/iloglob.pdf

International Organisation for Migration. (2011). *IOM Central Asia Operational Strategy 2011-2015.* International Organisation for Migration, Pp. 42.

IOM. (2011). *IOM Central Asia Operational Strategy 2011-2015.* International Organisation for Migration, Pp. 42.

Ives, JD and Messerli, B. (1989). *The Himalayan dilemma: Reconciling development and conservation.* London, UK: Routledge.

Jackson, N. (2006). International organizations, security dichotomies and the trafficking of persons and narcotics in post-Soviet Central Asia: a critique of the securitization framework. *Security Dialogue,* **37**(3): 299-317.

Jayaram, N. (2000). Sociology of youth in India. *In* M, S. Gore (Eds.), *Third survey of research in sociology and social anthropology,* (pp. 221-295). New Delhi: Indian Council of Social Science Research and Manak Publications.

Jayaram, N. (2009). Higher education in India: The challenges of change. *In* David, Palfreyman and Ted,

Trapper (Eds.), *Structuring mass higher education: The role of elite institutions,* (pp. 95-112). New Delhi: Routledge.

Jeffrey, C. (2008) 'Generation Nowhere': Rethinking Youth through the Lens of Unemployed Young Men'. *Progress in Human Geography, 32(6):* 739-58.

Jeffrey, C., and Mcdowell, L. (2004). Youth in a comparative perspective: Global change, local lives. *Youth & Society,* 36 (2), 131-142.

Jenkins, H., Lee, E., and Rodgers, G. (2007). *The quest for a fair globalisation three years on: Assessing the impact of the world commission on the social dimension of globalisation.* Geneva: ILO.

Jha, R. (2000). Reducing poverty and inequality in India: Has liberalisation helped? United Nations University: World Institute for Development Economics Research, Paper 204.

Jones, G. & Wallace, C. (1992) *Youth Family and Citizenship.* Buckingham: Open University Press.

Joshi, Kavita. (2003). *Sexuality in India: Teenager and teacher.* Gyan Books: India.

Kahanec, M., Zimmermann, K. (2008). *Migration and Globalization: Challenges and Perspectives for the Research Infrastructure.* Discussion Paper No. 3890. Germany: IZA, DIW Berlin, Bonn University and Free University Berlin. Pp 2-6.

Kapur, K. (1968). Youth Welfare, Encyclopaedia of Social Work in India, Vol.2, New Delhi, Planning Commission

Katageri, S. (2010). *An auto spy study of suicides among adolescents and young adults aged between 15—24 years in victoria hospital, bangalore medical college and research institute, bangalore.* (Unpublished Doctoral Dissertation) Department of Forensic Medicine, Bangalore Medical College and Research Institute, Bangalore: India.

Katz, H. C. (2000). *Converging divergences: Worldwide changes in employment systems.* Ithaca, NY: Cornell University Press.

Kazakhstan News Bulletin, (2005). *First Half of 2005 Shows a 9.1 Percent Growth in Economy, Plus 2 Percent Drop in Unemployment.* News Bulletin of the Embassy of the Republic of Kazakhstan to the USA and Canada, 5, 30. Washington DC, 2-3.

Kellner-Heinkele, B and Landau, J. (2011). *Language Politics in Contemporary Central Asia: National and Ethnic Identity and the Soviet Legacy.* I. B. Tauris.

Kelly, B. (2003). Globalisation and psychiatry. *Advances in Psychiatric Treatment,* 9, 464-70.

Khan, A. R., and Carl, R. (2001). *Inequality and poverty in China in the age of globalisation.* Oxford: Oxford University Press.

Kılavuz-T, I. (2009). Political and Social Networks in Tajikistan and Uzbekistan: 'Clan', Region and Beyond. *Central Asian Survey,* 28 (3): 323-334.

Kingdon, G. (2007). The progress of school education in India. In: Steven, B., Vincent, A., Anfara and Kathleen, R eds. *An International Look At Educating Young Adolescents,* Pp. 90-100. Information Age Publishing.

Kirmayer, L. J., & Minas, I. H. (2000). The future of cultural psychiatry: An international perspective. *Canadian Journal of Psychiatry*, 45, 438—446.

Koenig, M. (2001). Editorial. *International Journal on Multicultural Societies,* 3 (2):55.

Kohli S. and Narala, V. (2004). "Youth in Planned Development in India," *Social Change: Issues and Perspectives*, Vol. 34, No.2, 103—104

Koniordos, S. (2008). Social Capital Contested. *International Review of Sociology: Revue Internationale de Sociologie,* 18 (2): 317-337.

Kortum, E., and Ertel, M. (2003). Occupational stress and well-being at work: An overview of our current understanding and future directions. *African Newsletter on Occupational Health and Safety,* 13 (2), 35-8.

Kovalainen, A. (2004). 'Rethinking the Revival of Social Capital and Trust in Social Theory: Possibilities for Feminist Analyses of Social Capital and Trust.' *In:* Engendering the Social: Feminist Encounters with Social Theory (eds) B. L. Marshall and A. Witz, Open University Press, Maidenhead and New York.

Kristeva, J. (1990). 'The Adolescent Novel'. *In:* J. Forans and G. Bolin (Eds.), *Youth Culture in Late Modernity*. London, Sage, pp. 49-50.

Kuczynski, J., Eisenstadt, S.N., Boubakar L.Y. and Lotika, S., eds., (1988). *Perspectives on contemporary youth.* Hong Kong: United Nations University, 1-13.

Kuehnast, K., (2000). Coming of age in central Asia: dilemma and challenges facing youth and children. *Demokratizatsiya,* 8 (2), 186-90.

Kuhn, A. (1995) *Family Secrets: Acts of Memory and Imagination.* London: Verso.

Kunitz, S. J. (2000). Globalisation, states, and the health of indigenous peoples. *American Journal of Public Health,* 90, 1531-1539.

Kurian, N. J. (2007). Widening economic & social disparities: Implications for India. *Indian Journal of Medical Research,* 126, 374-380.

Kuznetsova, P. (2003). *Employment of the Population: Official and Unofficial Unemployment and its Impact on Poverty.* Paper presented at World Bank workshop on enhancing poverty monitoring in Azerbaijan, Kazakhstan and the Kyrgyz Republic, Issyk-Kol.

Kwong, J. (1985). Changing political culture and changing curriculum: An analysis of language textbooks in the people's republic of China. *Comparative Education,* 21, 197—208.

Lagree, J-C., (2004). Review essay: youth, families and global transformations. *Current Sociology,* 52 (1), 103-5.

Laitin, D. (1998). *Identity in Formation.* Ithaca: Cornell University Press.

Lakshminarayana, H. D. (1985). *College youth: Challenge and response.* New Delhi: Mittal Publications.

Landau, J and Kellner-Heinkele, B. (2001). *Politics of Language in the Ex-Soviet Muslim States: Azerbayjan,*

Uzbekistan, Kazakhstan, Kyrgyzstan, Turkmenistan, Tajikistan. London: Hurst and Company.

Lareau, A. (2003) *Unequal Childhoods: Class, Race and Family Life.* Berkeley: University of California Press.

Lash, S. (1994) 'Reflexivity and its Doubles: Structure, Aesthetics, Community'. In U. Beck, A. Giddens and S. Lash (Eds.) *Reflexive Modernization: Politics, Tradition and Aesthetics in the Modern Social Order* (pp. 110-73). Cambridge: Polity Press.

Lebedeva, M. (1997). *Novaia russkaia diaspora. Sotsial'no-psikhologicheskii analiz.* Moscow: RAN.

Lee, K. (2000). The impact of globalisation on public health: Implications for the UK faculty of public health medicine. *Journal of Public Health Medicine,* 22, 253-262.

Lehmann, W. (2007) 'I Just Don't Feel Like I Fit in: The Role of Habitus in University Drop-Out Decision'. *Canadian Journal of Higher Education, 37(2)*:89-110.

Li, H., Squire, L., Zou H. (1998). Explaining international and inter-temporal variations in income inequality. *Economic Journal,* 108, 26-43.

Li, Huijun and Prevatt, F. (2008). Fears and related anxieties in Chinese high school students. *School Psychology International,* 29 (1), 89-104.

Li, N., and Zhu, D. (2005). Mental health conditions of private high school students. *Chinese Journal of Special Education,* 65, 54-58.

Libin, Zhang. (2006). *Globalisation and its effects on youth employment in China.* Paper presented at Regional Expert

Group Meeting on Development Challenges for Young People. UNCC Bangkok, Institute for Labor Studies Ministry of Labor and Social Security of People's Republic of China.

Lin, J. (1993). *Education in post-mao China.* Westport, CT: Praeger.

Lloyd, B. C., Behrman, R. Jere., Stromquist, P. Nelly, and Cohen, B. ed. (2006). *The changing transitions to adulthood in developing countries: Selected studies* [online]. Retrieved from the National Academies Press at: http://www.nap.edu/catalog/11524.html

Loewenson, R. (2001). Globalisation and occupational health: A perspective from southern Africa. *Bulletin of the World Health Organisation,* 79 (9), 863-8.

Lopez, D. A., Mathers, D. C., Ezzati, M., Jamison, T. D., and Murray, J. L. C. (2006). *Global burden of disease and risk factors.* New York: Oxford University Press.

Mann, M. (1995). *A Political Theory of Nationalism and Its Excesses: Notions of Nationalism.* Eds. Sukumar Periwal. Budapest: Central European UP.

Mannheim, K. (1943). 'Diagnosis of Our Times,' (p.33). *In:* Lakshmi Narayana, H.D., 1985, *College Youth Challenge and Response,* Mittal Publications New Delhi, pp. 3-6.

Manning, N., and Patel, V., (2008). Globalisation and mental health: A special issue of global social policy. *Global Social Policy,* 8 (3), 299-300.

Maria. M. (2002). 'Youth in Southeast Asia: Living within the Continuity of Tradition and the Turbulence of Change'.

In: Brown, B., Larson, R. and Sarswathi, T.S., (Eds.), 2002. *The Worlds Youth: Adolescence in Eight Regions of the Globe.* Cambridge: Cambridge University Press, 171-206.

Mart, E. (2009). *Labour Migration in Central Asia: Implications of the Global Economic Crisis.* The Silk Road Studies Program, Institute for Security and Development Policy and Central Asia-Caucasus Institute. ISBN: 978-91-85937-57-8. Pp50.

Maurer-Fazio, M. (2003). Education as a determinant of lay-off, re-employment, and earnings in China's transitional labor market. In: E. Hannum and A. Park ed. *Education and Reform in China.* Cambridge, MA: Harvard University Press.

McDonough, P. (2000). Job insecurity and health. *International Journal of Health Services,* 30 (3), 453-76.

McGlinchey, E. (2006). *Regeneration or Degeneration? Youth Mobilization and the Future of Uzbek Politics.* Paper Papered for the National Bureau of Asian Research (NBR) Conference, June, 2006, Seattle: Washington.

McMichael and Beaglehole. (2000). The changing global context of public health. *Lancet, 356, 495-9.*

Michaud, J. (1996). A historical account of modern social change in Ladakh (Indian Kashmir) with special attention paid to tourism. *International Journal of Comparative Sociolog.* Vol. 37, pp. 286-301.

Miles, A. (1998). Women's bodies, women's selves: illness narratives and the 'Andean' body. *Body and Society,* 4, 1-19.

Misra, K. and Jain, M. (1975). *Youth, University and Community*, New Delhi, S. Chand and Company

Mittra, S and Kumar, B. (2004). *Encyclopaedia of Women in South Asia: Sri Lanka*. New Delhi: Gyan Publishing House, Vol. 5, Pp. 202-3.

Morch, Sve. (2003). Youth and education. *Young*, 11 (1), 49-73.

Nagaraj, R. (2000). Indian economy since 1980 virtuous growth or polarisation? *Economic and Political Weekly*, 35 (32), 2831-2839.

Nagaraj, R., A. Varoudakis and M-A. Veganzones. (2000). Long-term growth trends and convergence across Indian states. *Journal of International Development,* 12 (1), 45-70.

Nathan Light, N. (2011). Genealogy, History, Nation. *Nationalities Papers: The Journal of Nationalism and Ethnicity*, 39 (1): 33-53.

NCRB (National Crime Records Bureau). (2002). *Accidental deaths and suicides in India. Retrieved from* http://ncrb.nic.in/adsi/data/adsi2006/Suicides06.pdf

NCRB. (2005). *Accidental deaths and suicide in India*. Retrieved from: http://ncrb. nic.In /adsi/data/adsi 2005/home.htm

NCRB. (2007). *Accidental deaths and suicides in India. Retrieved from:*

Niyozov, S. (2001). *Education in Tajikistan: A Window to Understanding Change through Continuity.* Paper presented at the ANZCIES, Curtin University of Technology, Perth, WA.

Norberg—Hodge, H. (1991). *Ancient futures: Learning from Ladakh*. San Francisco, CA: Sierra Club Books.

O'Higgins, N. (2010). *Youth labour markets in Europe and central Asia.* Germany, Bonn University: Institute for the Study of Labour, Discussion Paper No. 5094, 32-3.

Out Look, The Weekly News Magazine, 27 May—2 June, 2008, Pp. 51-64.

Panda, R. (2009). Migration remittances: the emerging scenario. *India Quarterly: A Journal of International Affairs,* **65** (2): 167-83.

Patel, V. (2001). Poverty, inequality and mental health in developing countries, In D. A. Leon and G. Walt ed. *Poverty, Inequality and Health: An International Perspective,* pp. 247-62. Oxford: Oxford University Press.

Patel, V., and Kleinman, A. (2003). Poverty and common mental disorders in developing countries. *Bulletin of the World Health Organisation,* 81 (8), 609-15.

Patel, V., Araya, R., De-Lima, M., Ludermir, A., and Todd, C. (1999). Women, poverty and common mental disorders in four restructuring societies. *Social Science and Medicine,* 49 (11), 1461-72.

Paxton, W and Dixon, M. (2004) *State of the Nation: An Audit of Injustice in the UK.* London: IPPR.

Peyrouse, S. (2008). *The Russian Minority in Central Asia: Migration, Politics, and Language.* Occasional Papers, Kennan Institute, One Woodrow Wilson International Center for Scholars, Washington, D.C.

Phillips, Liu, Huaqing and Zhang, Y. (1999). Suicide and social change in China. *Culture Medicine and Psychiatry,* 23, 25-50.

Phillips, M. R., Yang, G., Zhang, Y., Wang, L., Ji, H., and Zhou, M. (2002b). Risk factors for suicide in China: A national case-control psychological autopsy study. *Lancet,* 360, 1728-1736.

Pickett, K., and Pearl, M. (2006). Multilevel analyses of neighbourhood socio-economic context and health outcomes: A critical review. *Journal of Epidemiology and Community Health,* 60 (2), 111-22.

Poppe, E. and Hagendoom, L. (2001). Types of Identifications among Russians in the Near Abroad. *Europe-Asia Studies,*1: 57-71.

Portes, A. (1997a). *Globalization from Below: The Rise of Transnational Communities.* Princeton, NJ: Princeton University Press.

Prince, M., Patel, V., Rahman, A. *et al.,* (2007). No health without mental health—A slogan with substance. *Lancet,* 370 (9590), 859-77.

Putnam, D. (2000) *Bowling Alone: The Collapse and Revival of American Community.* New York: Simon and Schuster.

Putnam, D. (1995b). Tuning in, Tuning out: the Strange Disappearance of Social Capital in America. *Political science and politics,* 28: 664-683.

Radio Free Asia (RFA). (2004, April 29). *China tries to redress age-old pressures on children.* Retrieved from: http://www. rfa.org/english/news/social/134677-20040429.htm l?Sear chterm=None

Radnitz, S. (2006). Weighing the Political and Economic Motivations for Migration in Post Soviet Space: The Case of Uzbekistan. *Europe-Asia Studies,* 58 (5): 653-77

Raj, K. N. (1990). Bridging rural—urban gap. *Economic and Political Weekly*, 25 (1), 25-27.

Rampal, Kuldip. (1999). Cultural bane or sociological boon? Impact of satellite television on urban youth in India. *In:* Vahya, Kamalipour and Kuldip, Rampal (Eds.), *Media, sex and drugs in the global village,* (pp. 115-30). New York: Rowman and Littlefield.

Rather, T. Ahmad and Bhat, M. Aslam (2011) 'Tribal Youth in Transition: A Discourse of Attitudes and Aspirations among Young People in Ladakh'. *Indian Journal of Youth Affairs, 15(2)*: 72-83.

Reay, D. (2005) 'Beyond Consciousness? The Psychic Landscape of Social Class'. *Sociology, 39(5)*:911-28.

Registrar Central and Census Commissioner. (2005). *Census India: Map Profile 2001 India: States and Union Territories*, New Delhi, Controller Publication

Reynolds, P. (1991). *Dance, civet cat: child labour in the Zambezi valley.* Athens, OH: Ohio University Press.

Reynolds, T. (2010). Transnational Family Relationships, Social Networks and Return Migration among British-Caribbean Young People. *Ethnic and Racial Studies,* 33 (5): 797-815.

Rigi, J. (2003). The conditions of post-soviet dispossessed youth and work in Almaty, Kazakhstan. *Critique of Anthropology,* 23 (1), 35-6.

Rizvi, J. (1996). *Ladakh: Crossroads of high Asia*. New Delhi, India: Oxford University Press.

Rizvi, J. (1999). *Trans—Himalayan caravans: Merchant princes and peasant traders in Ladakh*. New Delhi, India: Oxford University Press.

Roberts, K. (2009). Young People's Education to Work Transitions and the Inter-generational Social Mobility in Post-Soviet Central Asia. *Young* 17 (1):59-80.

Roberts, K. (2010). Post-Communist Youth: is there a Central Asian pattern? *Central Asian Survey,* 29(4): 541.

Roberts, S. (2010). 'Misrepresenting 'Choice Biographies'?: A Reply to Woodman'. *Journal of Youth Studies, 13(1)*: 137-49.

Roberts, S. (2012). 'One Step Forward, One Step Beck: A Contribution to the Ongoing Conceptual Debate in Youth Studies'. *Journal of Youth Studies, 15(3)*: 389-401.

Royse, S and Verghese, C. (2007). *Social Welfare,* July 2007, vol. 54, No. 4, PP. 33-36.

Rychen, S. and Salganik, H. (2003). *Key Competencies for a Successful Life in a Well-Functioning Society.* Cambridge: Hogrefe and Huber.

Sagar, Ahluwalia. (1972). *Youth in revolt.* Young Asia Publications: New Delhi. P. 3.

Saidazimova, G. (2005). *Women and power in Central Asia: The struggle for equal rights.* Available at: http://www.payvand.com/news/05/dec/1239.html (accessed 12 June 2010).

Sampson, E. (1989). The challenge of social change for psychology. *American Psychologist,* 44, 914-921.

Sanderson, M and Kentor, J. (2008). Foreign Direct Investment and International Migration: A Cross-National Analysis of Less-Developed Countries, 1985-2000. *International Sociology,* 23(4): 514-539.

Sanjiv, K., Rahul, S., and N. K. Saini. (2010). Depression, anxiety and stress among adolescent students belonging to affluent families: A school-based study. *Indian J Pediatr,* 77 (2), 161-165.

Sarkar, S. N. (1974). *Student unrest: A social psychology study.* Calcutta: India Book House.

Saxena, S., Thornicroft, G., Knapp, M., Whiteford, H. (2007). Resources for mental health: Scarcity, in equity and inefficiency. *The Lancet,* 370, 878-89.

Sayer, A. (2005) *The Moral Significance of Class.* Cambridge: University Press.

Schlyter, B. (2001). Language Policies in Present-Day Central Asia. *International Journal on Multicultural Societies,* 3 (2): 127-36.

Scott, J. (2002) 'Social Class and Stratification in Late Modernity'. *Acta Sociologica, 15(1):* 23-35.

Shah, B. V. (1964). *Social change and college students of Gujarat.* M. S. University: Baroda, India

Shanahan, M., Mortimer, J., and Kru"ger, H. (2002). 'Adolescence and adult work in the twentyfirst century'. *In:* B. Brown, R.W. Larson and T.S. Sarswathi, eds. *The worlds youth: adolescence in eight regions of the globe.* Cambridge: Cambridge University Press, 11.

Shariff, Aabusaleh. (2007 November 22). Problems of numbers: Skills shortage could scupper high growth rates. *The Times of India*. P. 12.

Shen, Q., Lu, Y., Hu, C., Deng, X., Gao, H., Huang, X. *et al.,* (1998). A preliminary study of the mental health of young migrant workers in shenzhen. *Psychiatry and Clinical Neurosciences*, 52, 370-373. [PubMed: 9895197].

Sing, A., Lal, A., and Shekhar. (2010). Prevalence of depression among medical students of a private medical college in India. *Online Journal of Health and Allied Sciences,* 9 (4), 1-3.l

Sing, L. B., Sing, A. K., and Rani, A. (1996). Level of self-concepts in educated unemployed young men in India: An empirical analysis. *Journal of Economic Psychology*, 17 (5), 639-43.

Singh, K. S. (1992). *People of India: An introduction.* Anthropological Survey of India, Seagull Books: Culcutta.

Skeldon, R. (1985). Population pressure, mobility, and socio—economic change in mountainous environments: Regions of refuge in comparative perspective. *Mountain Research and Development.* Vol. 5, pp. 233-250.

Smith, G., Law, V., Wilson, A., Bohr, A and Allworth, E. (1998). *Nation-Building in the Post-Soviet Borderlands: The Politics of National Identities.* Cambridge: Cambridge University Press.

State Statistics Bureau of China (SSBC). (2005). *Statistics yearbook, various years.* Retrieved from: http://chinadataonline.org/

Stiglitz, J. E. (2002). *Globalisation and its discontents.* New York: W.W. Norton & Company.

Svendsen, H. (2006). Studying Social Capital in Situ: a Qualitative Approach. *Theory and society,* 35: 39-70.

Swartz, D. (1997) *Culture and Power: The Sociology of Pierre Bourdieu.* Chicago: Chicago University Press.

Sweetman, P. (2003) 'Twenty-first Century Dis-ease? Habitual Reflexivity or the Reflexive Habitus'. *Sociological Review, 51(4)*:528-49.

Teese, V. (2000) *Academic Success and Social Power: Examinations and Inequality.* Carlton: Melbourne University Press.

Tennant, C. (2001). Work-related stress and depressive disorders. *Journal of Psychosomatic Research,* 51(5), 697-704.

The Times of India. (2007, April 25). *HSBC survey: wealth brings happiness, say Mumbai, Shanghai.* Retrieved from: www.timesofindia.com

The Times of India. (2009, March 19). *Vacant: Ideas to create jobs.* Retrieved from: www.timesofindia.com

The Week. (September 16, 2007) pp. 32-43.

Thieme, S. (2007). *Osh-Bishkek-Almaty-Moscow and Return? How Different Generations Sustain their Livelihoods in Multilocal Settings.* Bishkek: Social Research Center, American University of Central Asia.

Thornicroft, G. *et al.* (2009). Global pattern of experienced and anticipated discrimination against people with schizophrenia: A cross-sectional survey. *The Lancet,* 373, 408-415.

Threadgold, S. and Nilan, P. (2009). 'Reflexivity of Contemporary Youth, Risk and Cultural Capital'. *Current Sociology, 57(1)*: 47—50.

Tonelli, S. (2009). Migration and democracy in Central and Eastern Europe. *Transfer: European Review of Labour and Research,* **9**: 483-502.

Tonelli, S. 2003. Migration and Democracy in Central and Eastern Europe. *Transfer: European Review of Labour and Research,* 9: 483-502.

Trilling, D. (2009). From Central Asia and back. *World Policy Journal,* **26** (1):79.

Trilling, D. (2009). Tajikistan: Dushanbe Confronts Dysfunction in Education Seector. Available from: www.eurasianet.org [Accessed 12 June 2011].

UNAIDS. (2008). *Report on the global aids epidemic, United Nations programme on HIV/AIDS,* (UNAIDS). ISBN 9789291737178. Available from: www.unaids.org [Accessed, 13 April 2011].

UNDP. (2003). *Millennium Development Goals: National Reports. A Look through a Gender Lens.* New York: United Nations.

United Nations (UN). (2005). *World youth report 2005.* Retrieved from: http:// (Accessed Dec. 2009).

United Nations. (1986). *The Situation of Youth in the 1980's and Prospects and Challenges for the Year 2000.* New York, PP. 10-11.

United Nations. (2005). *World Youth Report 2005.* New York: United Nations.

Van Beek, Martijn. (2003). The art of representation: Domesticating Ladakhi identity. *In* Marie, Lecomte-Tilouine and Pascale, Dollfus (Eds.), *Ethnic revival and religious turmoil: Identities and representations in the Himalayas*, (pp. 283-301). New Delhi: Oxford University Press.

Verma, S., Sharma, D., and Larson, W. Reed. (2002). School stress in India: Effects on time and daily emotions. *International Journal of Behavioural Development,* 26 (6), 500-508.

Wagner, Helmut. (2002). *Globalisation and unemployment.* Springer, Publication, Pp. 401.

Wang, F. (2002). Rural migrants in shanghai: Living under the shadow of socialism. *International Migration Review,* 36 (2), 520-546.

Waters, M. (1994). *Modern Sociological Theory.* London: Sage.

Watt, D. and Roessingh, H. (2001). The Dynamics of ESL Dropout: Plus Ca change. *Canadian Modern Language Review,* 58(2): 203-222.

Weber, Max (1978 [1920]) 'Status Groups and Classes'. In G. Roth and C. Wittich (Eds.) *Economy and Society* (pp. 301-7). Berkeley: University of California Press.

Weitz, R. 2008. *Central Asia: Looking at Language Politics.* Available online at: (accessed 5 0ct. 2012).

WHO (World Health Organisation). (2005a). *Mental health atlas.* Geneva: WHO.

WHO. (2004). *Prevention of mental disorders: Effective interventions and policy options.* Geneva: WHO.

WHO. (2000). *Preventing suicide: A resource for primary health care workers.* WHO/MNH/ MBD/00.4. Geneva: WHO. Retrieved from: www.who.int/mentalhealth/media / en/59.pdf.

WHO. (2006). *Global plan of action on workers' health 2008-2017: Draft for external consultation.* Geneva: WHO.

WHO. (2009). *Mental health, poverty and development.* ECOSOC Meeting, Addressing non Communicable Diseases and Mental Health: Major Challenges to Sustainable Development in the 21st century. WHO Discussion Paper July 2009.

Winefield, Anthony H. (2002). Unemployment, underemployment, occupational stress and psychological well-being. *Australian Journal of Management,* 27, 137-48.

Wong, D. F., HE, X. *et. al.,* (2008). Mental health of migrant workers in China: Prevalence and correlates. *Soc Psychiatry Psychiatr Epidemiol,* 43 (6), 483-9.

Woodman, D. (2009) 'The Mysterious Case of the Pervasive Choice Biography: Ulrich Beck, Structure/Agency, and the Middling State of Theory in the Sociology of Youth'. *Journal of Youth Studies,12(3):* 243-56.

Woodman, D. (2010) 'Class, Individualisation and Tracing Processes of Inequality in a Changing World: A Reply to Steven Roberts'. *Journal of Youth Studies, 13(6)*: 737-47.

World Bank. (2007). *World development report.* Retrieved from. And http://devdata.worldbank.org/hnpstats/ dp1. as p (accessed Sept. 2009).

World Bank. (2003). *Youth Development and Peace Conference: Compact Report.* France, Paris: World Bank.

World Bank. (2007a). *World Development Report 2007: Development and the Next Generation.* Washington DC: The World Bank.

World Bank. (2007b). *Young People in Eastern Europe and Central Asia: from Policy to Action.* Conference Background Paper, May 21-24, Rome: Italy.

Wortley, H. (2006). *Depression, a leading contributor to global burden of disease.* Washington DC: Population Reference Bureau. Retrieved from: http://www.prb.org

Wu, HX., and Zhou, L. (1996). Rural-to-urban migration in China. *Asian-Pacific Economic Literature,* 10, 54-67 [PubMed: 12292973].

Wulff, H. (1995) 'Introducing Youth Culture in its Own Right: The State of the Art and New Possibilities'. *In:* V. Amit-Talai and H. Wulff (Eds.) *Youth Cultures: A Cross Cultural Perspective* (pp. 10-11). London and New York: Routledge.

Yan, Yunxiang. (2006). Little emperors or frail pragmatists? China's 80ers generation. *Current History,* 105 (692), 255-63.

Yang, Wang. (2005, Oct. 24). High saving rate indicates dangers of capital flight. *Xinhua Net.* Retrieved from: http://jjckb.xinhuanet.com/www/article/200510 24104534-1.shtml

Yedla, C. (1992). *Global Youth, Peace and Development: The Role of Science and Technology in the Contemporary Society* (Vol. II). Ajanta Publications India, p. 29-48

Yedla, C. (1989). *Youth in the Contemporary World*, New Delhi, Mittal Publications.

Yip, K. (2006). Community mental health in the people's republic of China: A critical analysis. *Community Mental Health Journal,* 42 (1), 41-51.

Zhakenov, G. (2006). Kazakhstan National Report on Higher Education System Development. Available from: www.unesco.kz/he/kazakh_eng.htm [Accessed 15 May 2010].

Zhang, J. Xiao, Shuiyuan and L. Zhou. (2010). Mental disorders and suicide among young rural Chinese: A case-control psychological autopsy study. *American Journal of Psychiatry*, 167, 773-81.

Ziyaeva, D. (2006). "Changing Identities among Uzbek Youth: Transition from Regional to Socio-economic Identities." Paper Prepared for the National Bureau of Asian Research (NBR) Conference On *Generational Change and Leadership Succession in Uzbekistan.* Seattle: Washington D.C.

Zontini, E. (2004b). Immigrant Women in Barcelona: Coping with the Consequences of Transnational Lives. *Journal of Ethnic and Migration Studies*, 30 (6): 1113-1144.

APPENDIX

INTERVIEW SCHEDULE

For

Field Study in Ladakh

1. PERSONAL DATA:

1.1 Name _____

1.2 Sex: Male/ Female

1.3 Age _____

1.4 Religion:

    a. Muslim: Sunni/ Shia _____

    b. Hindu _____

    c. Buddhist _____

    d. Jain _____

    e. Sikh _____

    f. Christian _____

    g. Other _____

1.5 Address:

Rural/ Urban

a. Village_____

b. Town_____

1.6 Current residence:

a. Daily commuter from the village _____

b. Living in town with relatives _____

c. Living in hostel/ rented room _____

d. Any other (specify) _____

1.7 Educational level:

a. Illiterate _____

b. Primary _____

c. Middle _____

d. Hr. Secondary _____

e. Graduate _____

f. Post Graduate _____

g. Any other (specify) _____

1.8 Occupation:

a. Student _____

b. Daily labourer _____

c. Petty trader _____

d. Self employed _____

e. Govt. employee _____

f. Private employee _____

g. Farmer _____

h. Unemployed _____

i. Any other (specify) _____

1.9 Monthly income _____

1.10 Marital status:

    a. Married _____

    b. Unmarried _____

1.11 Type of the family you belong to:

    a. Nuclear family _____

    b. Joint family _____

    c. Extended family _____

1.12 Fathers/ Guardians education _____

1.13 Fathers/ Guardians occupation _____

1.14 Fathers/ Guardians income _____

2.

2.1 Education for you means?

    a. Technical and Professional education _____

    b. Academic education _____

    c. Religious education _____

    d. Any other (specify) _____

2.2 If, technical, professional and academic education, why?

    a. Provides higher Govt. job opportunities _____

    b. Trains in skills that are required by the economy _____

    c. Gives high status in society _____

    d. Encourages the spirit of competition _____

    e. Any other (specify) _____

2.3 If, religious education, why? _____

    a. Brings purity in thought and action _____

    b. Emphasis on equality in society _____

    c. Provides peace of mind _____

    d. Any other (specify) _____

2.4 If you have the wish to study further, but your parents do not approve it. Do you then,

    a. Give up your wish to respect the parent's advice _____

    b. Explain the genuineness and reasonableness of your wish _____

    c. Tell your parents that it is their duty to provide for your studies _____

    d. Any other (specify) _____

2.5 What do you do in your leisure time in college/ work place?

    a. Gossip _____

    b. Play _____

    c. Eat and drink in canteen/ hotel _____

    d. Take solitude _____

    e. Visit library _____

    f. Any other (specify) _____

2.6 What is your best occupational choice?

    a. Govt. job _____

    b. Business _____

    c. Private sector job _____

    d. Traditional parental occupation _____

    e. Agricultural _____

    f. Any other (specify) _____

2.7 If Govt. job, why?

    a. Better job security _____

    b. Retirement benefits _____

    c. Less strictness _____

2.8 If Business, why?

    a. Hereditary _____

    b. Enables to earn more money _____

    c. Gives personal satisfaction _____

    d. Any other (specify) _____

2.9 If Private sector job, why?

    a. Sound salary _____

    b. No other option _____

    c. Any other (specify) _____

2.10 If the opportunity comes, will you work?

    a. Abroad _____

    b. Within locality _____

    c. Outside locality _____

    d. Any other (specify) _____

2.11 If, abroad, why?

    a. To earn more money _____

    b. To achieve high Status _____

    c. To keep pace with modern western life _____

    d. Any other (specify) _____

2.12 Given an easy chance, for which purpose, you would like to take a loan?

    a. Business _____

    b. Education_____

    c. Vehicle_____

    d. House _____

    e. Any other (specify) _____

2.13 Do you think tourism has created alternative job opportunities in this locality?

    a. Yes _____

    b. No _____

    c. Do not know _____

2.14. If, yes, have you any time worked as a tourist guide?

    a. Yes _____

    b. No _____

2.15 What is your opinion about tourism in Ladakh?

    a. Positive _____

    b. Negative _____

    c. Mixed _____

    d. No opinion _____

2.16 If, positive, reasons:

    a. Provides job opportunity _____

    b. Enables to interact with people
       of different cultures _____

    c. Gives Exposure to local goods
       and products _____

    d. Any other (specify) _____

2.17 If, negative, reasons:

    a. Pollutes local environment _____

    b. Undermines local culture _____

    c. Encourages drug addiction among
       youth _____

    d. Any other (specify) _____

2.18 Do you think young people are more international in spirit and behaviour than older generation?

    a. Yes _____

    b. No _____

    c. Do not know _____

2.19 If, yes, what kind of information, you daily keep about the world?

    a. Economic information _____

    b. Political information _____

    c. Business information _____

    d. Games and sports information _____

    e. Bollywood/ Hollywood information _____

    f. Any other (specify) _____

2.20 Which of these items do you personally own?

    a. Music _____

    b. Cell phone _____

    c. Two wheeler _____

    d. PC/laptop _____

    e. Do not own any item _____

2.21 Do you listen/ watch radio and T.V?

    a. Yes daily _____

    b. Once or twice a week _____

    c. Not interested _____

2.22 If, yes, which kind of programs you prefer most?

    a. Indian films/ musical programmes _____

    b. Folk films/ musical programmes _____

    c. Western films/ musical programmes _____

    d. Any other (specify) _____

2.23 If, educated, do you read newspaper and magazines?

    a. Yes, daily _____

    b. Once or twice a week _____

    c. Not interested _____

2.24 If, yes, what kind of magazines and newspapers you read mostly?

    a. Science magazines and papers _____

    b. Film Magazines and papers _____

    c. Current affair magazines and papers _____

    d. Fiction magazines and papers _____

    e. Any other (specify) _____

2.25 What is your opinion about communication media like press, radio, T.V etc.?

    a. Positive _____

    b. Negative _____

    c. Mixed _____

    d. No opinion _____

2.26 If, positive, reasons:

    a. Gives useful information _____

    b. Entertains _____

    c. Presents true picture of reality _____

    d. Any other (specify) _____

2.27 If, negative, reasons:

    a. Disturbs your studies _____

    b. Minimizes interaction with relatives and friends _____

    c. Raises expectations which can't be fulfilled _____

    d. Encourages crime and violence
        in society _____

    e. Undermines your local culture
        and tradition _____

    f. Advertises goods which you
        can't buy _____

    g. Encourages individualism _____

    h. Any other (specify) _____

2.28 Do you feel that youth in Ladakh indicates separate image of their selves from adult society?

    a. Yes _____

    b. No _____

    c. Do not know _____

2.29 If, yes, what is the generally adopted image of self?

    a. Idealistic _____

    b. Materialistic _____

    c. Industrious _____

    d. Lazy _____

    e. Romantic _____

    f. Selfish _____

    g. Wise _____

    h. Any other (specify) _____

2.30 Which type of family do you prefer most?

    a. Joint family _____

    b. Nuclear family _____

2.31 If, joint family, reasons:

    a. Encourages social control _____

    b. Promotes co-operative virtues _____

    c. Provides psychological security _____

    d. Any other (specify) _____

2.32 If, nuclear family, reasons:

    a. Gives more socio-economic freedom _____

    b. Provides better procreation and socialization to children _____

    c. Favours controlled reproduction _____

    d. Any other (specify) _____

2.33 Do you think that men and women should be given equal status and opportunity?

    a. Yes _____

    b. No _____

2.34 If, yes, why?

    a. It will lead to a sound society _____

    b. Enable women to tackle socio-economic problems _____

    c. Reduce crime rate against women _____

    d. Any other (specify) _____

2.35 If, no, why?

    a. Increase crime rate against women _____

    b. Destroy religious and moral fabric _____

    c. Increase unemployment among men _____

    d. Any other (specify) _____

2.36 On which issue do you differ most with your parents?

    a. Money matters _____

    b. Religious beliefs _____

    c. Political beliefs _____

    d. Friendship matters _____

    e. Any other (specify) _____

2.37 If, on money matters, reasons:

    a. Do not give you enough money _____

    b. Do not allow you to consume costly
        and big brand items _____

    c. Any other (specify) _____

2.38 If, on religious beliefs, reasons:

    a. Force you to perform certain religious rites
        much unreasonable and against your will
        and conviction _____

    b. Force you to visit a place of worship
        frequently _____

    c. Any other (specify) _____

2.39 If, on political beliefs, reasons:

    a. Consider religion important in politics _____

    b. Believe in dynastic politics _____

    c. Do not allow you to participate in
        political affairs _____

    d. Any other (specify) _____

2.40 If, on friendship, reasons:

    a. Consider friendship with opposite
        sex against morality _____

    b. Do not allow you to spend much
        time with friends' _____

    c. Don not allow you to bring friends
        at home _____

    d. Any other (specify) _____

2.41 Which activities you mostly share with your friends?

    a. Gossip _____

    b. Watch T.V _____

    c. Roaming around town _____

    d. Study together _____

    e. Play cards _____

    f. Any other (specify) _____

2.42 Do you have girl/ boy friend?

    a. Yes _____

    b. No _____

2.43 If, no, reasons?

    a. It is against religious codes _____

    b. Parents do not like _____

    c. Increase social disorder _____

    d. Not interested _____

    e. Any other (specify) _____

2.44 Do you think virginity is a virtue?

    a. Yes _____

    b. No _____

2.45 If, no, do you think premarital sex is:

    a. Not so much a moral issue _____

    b. Experimenting with sex _____

    c. All about being comfortable with
        the person one loves _____

    d. Any other (specify) _____

2.46 Do you think that elders of the society should not interfere in the affairs of young people?

    a. Yes _____

    b. No _____

2.47 If, Yes, are you individually deciding about your daily life and future?

    a. Yes _____

    b. No _____

2.48 Do you favour the use of violence to bring about change in society?

    a. Yes _____

    b. No _____

2.49 If, Yes, which one of the activities you have participated?

    a. Political strikes _____

    b. Student strikes _____

    c. General strikes _____

    d. Any other (specify) _____

2.50 Have you been any time arrested by police?

    a. Yes _____

    b. No _____

2.51 If, yes, reasons:

    a. Plundered public/ govt./

       private property _____

    b. Consumed drugs _____

    c. Quarrelled with administrators/

       bureaucrats _____

    d. Any other (specify) _____

2.52 Then, who released you on bail, from the police custody?

 a. Friends _____

 b. Parents _____

 c. Relatives _____

 d. Any other (specify) _____

2.53 What is your opinion for age a person should marry?

 a. 18-21 years' _____

 b. 22-25 years' _____

 c. 25 & above years _____

 d. Any other (specify) _____

2.54 Suppose you are in love with a person from any other religion, but your parents and relatives do not allow you to marry him/ her. Would you then change your religion to marry the person you love?

 a. Yes _____

 b. No _____

2.55 If, yes, why?

 a. Do not consider religious important in marriage making _____

 b. Do not bother about the parents and relatives wish _____

 c. Want to encourage inter-religion marriages _____

 d. Any other (specify) _____

2.56 If, no, why?

    a. Consider religion more important _____

    b. Can not go against parents and
       relatives wish _____

    c. Any other (specify) _____

2.57 Which dress pattern and food habits you prefer most?

    a. Local _____

    b. Western _____

    c. Any other (specify) _____

2.58 If, local, reasons:

    a. More suitable according to the
       climatic conditions _____

    b. More interesting and superior
       than others _____

    c. Any other (specify) _____

2.59 If, western, reasons:

    a. Makes you feel enlightened
       and superior _____

    b. More comfortable and superior
       than local _____

    c. Any other (specify) _____

2.60 To make your appearance more beautiful and fashionable, will you willingly pay for costly and big brand items?

    a. Yes _____

    b. No _____

2.61 Do, you:

    a. Always obey your parents' _____

    b. Obey them whenever you agree
       with them _____

    c. Do not obey your parents as they
       belong to older generation _____

    d. Any other (specify) _____

2.62 Suppose you and your friends have decided to do any work, but the elders of your community are displeased at this as they consider it anti social. Do you then:

    a. Stop working _____

    b. Ignore the advice of elders and continue
       the work _____

    c. Any other (specify) _____

3.

3.1 Observations of the research investigator:

_____

_____

_____

_____

_____

_____

_____

_____

_____

_____

Place _____

Date _____

Investigators name _____

Signature _____

Remarks of supervisor:

_____

_____

_____

_____

_____